MW00682163

KL JUL 2011

LOVE

NOT
SMOKING

Hay House Titles of Related Interest

YOU CAN HEAL YOUR LIFE, the movie,
starring Louise L. Hay & Friends
(available as a 1-DVD program and an expanded 2-DVD set)
Watch the trailer at: **www.LouiseHayMovie.com**

THE SHIFT, the movie, starring Dr. Wayne W. Dyer
(available as a 1-DVD program and an expanded 2-DVD set)
Watch the trailer at: **www.DyerMovie.com**

AM I BEING KIND: How Asking One Simple
Question Can Change Your Life . . . and Your World,
by Michael J. Chase

A BURNING DESIRE: Dharma God and the
Path of Recovery, by Kevin Griffin

A COURSE IN WEIGHT LOSS, by Marianne Williamson

EXCUSES BEGONE!: How to Change Lifelong,
Self-Defeating Thinking Habits, by Dr. Wayne W. Dyer

THE SECRET OF INSTANT HEALING,
by Dr. Frank J. Kinslow

STOP PAIN: Relieve Inflammation for an Active Life,
by Vijay Vad, M.D.

YOU CAN HEAL YOUR LIFE, by Louise L. Hay

All of the above are available at your local bookstore,
or may be ordered by visiting:

Hay House USA: **www.hayhouse.com**®
Hay House Australia: **www.hayhouse.com.au**
Hay House UK: **www.hayhouse.co.uk**
Hay House South Africa: **www.hayhouse.co.za**
Hay House India: **www.hayhouse.co.in**

LOVE

NOT

SMOKING

PROFESSOR KAREN PINE & PROFESSOR BEN [C] FLETCHER

HAY HOUSE, INC.
Carlsbad, California • New York City
London • Sydney • Johannesburg
Vancouver • Hong Kong • New Delhi

Copyright © 2011 by Ben [C] Fletcher and Karen Pine

Published and distributed in the United States by: Hay House, Inc.: www.hayhouse.com • **Published and distributed in Australia by:** Hay House Australia Pty. Ltd.: www.hayhouse.com.au • **Published and distributed in the United Kingdom by:** Hay House UK, Ltd.: www.hayhouse.co.uk • **Published and distributed in the Republic of South Africa by:** Hay House SA (Pty), Ltd.: www.hayhouse.co.za • **Distributed in Canada by:** Raincoast: www.raincoast.com • **Published in India by:** Hay House Publishers India: www.hayhouse.co.in

All rights reserved. No part of this book may be reproduced by any mechanical, photographic, or electronic process, or in the form of a phonographic recording; nor may it be stored in a retrieval system, transmitted, or otherwise be copied for public or private use—other than for "fair use" as brief quotations embodied in articles and reviews—without prior written permission of the publisher.

The authors of this book do not dispense medical advice or prescribe the use of any technique as a form of treatment for physical, emotional, or medical problems without the advice of a physician, either directly or indirectly. The intent of the authors is only to offer information of a general nature to help you in your quest for emotional and spiritual well-being. In the event you use any of the information in this book for yourself, which is your constitutional right, the authors and the publisher assume no responsibility for your actions.

Library of Congress Control Number: 2010941916

ISBN: 978-1-4019-3192-6

14 13 12 11   4 3 2 1
1st edition, May 2011

Printed in the United States of America

From the Editor: To our North American readers, please note that for the most part, we have maintained the British style of spelling, grammar, punctuation, and syntax of the original text in order to preserve the editorial intent of the authors, who hail from the United Kingdom.

*purchased at the thrift shop on Ellis..

STOP IN THE NAME OF LOVE

To: Gussie

From: Augustina ♡

I have bought you this book because: it's been

too long. Smoking is gross.

It is not good for your health.

Look at your face. Think of

all the money spent on

cigarettes. I know it's been

the most comfortable crutch...

but it's time to rise up and
do this 🌞✝

CONTENTS

ACKNOWLEDGEMENTS

There are a number of people to whom we owe a huge debt of gratitude in making this book possible. First of all to Ronel Erasmus who has been overseeing the running of this quit-smoking programme in our community projects, where Do Something Different has been improving the health and wellbeing of thousands of people. Ronel's sheer enthusiasm, positive energy and endless passion for DSD brighten the lives of those who come into contact with her. She is a huge inspiration to all and we are so grateful to have her in our lives. We'd also like to express our sincere thanks to Poppy Elston and Lucille Omurcan for delivering the Love Not Smoking: Do Something Different message and helping people to quit smoking and move on with their lives. Special thanks also go to Anna Mertziani for playing an important role in helping to develop and test this programme. And to her and Neil Howlett for their rigorous research and attention to detail, which have made a vital contribution to the scientific rigour of the programme. We also have to say a huge thank you to the many ex-smokers who have worked through the programme and given us their full support and confidence in its unrivalled success. To Keith Powell especially, for grasping the DSD message to his heart and for giving something back to others. And to the West Norfolk partnership, including Ian Burbridge and Martin Slater, for having the vision and foresight to bring Do Something Different to the people they serve and support. Thank you. And thanks also to many other friends who have made DSD a part of their personal or professional lives, including Shivani Sharma, Pete Burden, Simonne Gnessen, Ray Richards, Karen Durkin, Angela Cooke, Tom Nixon, Will McInnes, Alex Davda, Gary Kupshik, Paul Mullin and Jessica Chivers.

We would also like to thank our agent Sheila Crowley for all her encouragement, support and belief in our work. And, last but not least, the fabulous team at Hay House for bringing their professionalism and wealth of experience and knowledge to this publication. And for having a caring and enlightened ethos that aligns perfectly with our mission to continue to help people to lead better lives.

Part I

ALL ABOUT THE LOVE NOT SMOKING: DO SOMETHING DIFFERENT PROGRAMME

Chapter 1

WHAT IS THE LOVE NOT SMOKING: DO SOMETHING DIFFERENT PROGRAMME?

Welcome to a refreshing new approach to quitting smoking. Whether this is the first time you've tried to ditch the habit or you're a serial quitter, we think you'll love Love Not Smoking. The techniques in this book, which you'll get to know and live by, are based on the powerful Do Something Different principles we have developed in our work as psychology professors and human behaviour analysts. And, best of all, they work.

The Love Not Smoking: Do Something Different method makes use of the science behind why people get trapped by or stuck with particular habits. It's a pioneering technique that helps people break free from all sorts of addictions. It has been tried and tested, and brings with it success stories from many walks of life. Now you have the chance to learn this technique, one that will painlessly release you from the grip of your own unwanted behaviours. This method helps people really get what they want from life. To be no longer the victim of habits and addictions. More importantly, to stop living life on autopilot.

The success of this technique, and 21st-century scientific research, has begun to change the way people think about unwanted behaviour, addiction and habit. For a long time scientists have known that there is a 'pathway' in the brain behind everything we do, a set of interconnected brain cells that form a path along which messages travel. And the more they travel along it, the more that pathway gets hard-wired into the brain. We're excited by recent research which has shown that, at any age or stage of life, human beings can forge new brain pathways. The brain may have designated neural connections but they are not fixed at birth, nor are they necessarily with us for life. They can be modified and new ones can be formed. That's the key to change. We believe that when people replace old brain patterns with new ones, there is far less chance of them repeating the mistakes of the past. Because the old habits were encoded in those redundant brain pathways, in that old wiring. The powerful Do Something Different technique teaches new behaviours that forge new pathways.

The upshot is this: not only does the brain affect what we do; what we do also affects the brain. And so, of course, when we Do Something Different, we get something different. That's why behavioural techniques like this one are so incredibly effective and powerful. You may be addicted to nicotine, but your brain is far more addicted to life – or at least to all the sneaky, automatic rituals and routines that are hooked up to your smoking habit. The cup of coffee, the long drive, the telephone calls, the stressful conversation – all those well-established triggers. Do Something Different is a skill that you can develop, practise and incorporate into your everyday life. With amazing results. You see, it's more than just a quit-smoking programme. Even though it will help you give up smoking, it's also a personal development programme.

We first introduced this technique in the successful *The No Diet Diet: Do Something Different* book, a bestseller now published in 23 languages worldwide. By using Do Something Different, people everywhere – including serial dieters who'd struggled for years to fight the flab – found it easy to lose weight. They reprogrammed their wiring with new behaviours and reconditioned themselves so they were no longer slaves to their old ways. They unlearned the habits of the past, which had led to overeating, and replaced them with new healthier, positive ones. They lost weight but also found a new zest for life, a new energy and confidence. Do Something Different has also released people from the stranglehold of stress and anxiety, and has turned around the lives of thousands of people, both personally and professionally. As psychologists we think we have more than an inkling about the psychology of the smoker, so...

> **Everyone who has tried the Do Something Different method has been shocked at how easy it is. They love not smoking. And their loved ones love them not smoking.**

This comes as no surprise: the Do Something Different approach gives the quitter new life habits that replace smoking, so of course they don't miss it. Positive addictions take over from the old ways. The ex-smokers have gained something, not had anything taken away. Crazy as it may seem, when a smoker's brain has been hijacked by nicotine, they convince themselves that the next cigarette is the high spot on their future horizon, the one pleasure they have to look forward to (even though the pleasure comes from relief of withdrawal from nicotine). It seems bizarre that anyone should eagerly anticipate something with potentially fatal consequences, but the habitual brain isn't always a rational one. And for some people, whose lives are deprived or unhappy, smoking is perceived as their 'one pleasure' and they use this false sense of entitlement to justify continuing.

Behavioural and Psychological Addictions Are Stronger Than Nicotine Addiction

This programme helps to change this flawed reasoning. It does this by resetting the faulty anticipation–reward cycle by imposing behavioural-blockers and positive substitutes. This works because, in fact, behavioural and psychological addictions are far stronger than nicotine addiction. So, rather than taking something *away* from the quitter, Do Something Different helps them to *add* something. To quote the words of the grand master of quitting, Allen Carr (more about how our approach differs from his in Chapter 4), smoking doesn't fill the void, it creates it. Do Something Different helps you avoid the void.

People who have given up with this method tell us they love not smoking. You might ask why it took decades of scientific research to come up with something so simple. That's because the human mind is sophisticated and the science behind the method is complex. But the solution is simple. And if you want to stop smoking, that's all that matters.

Simple Changes Make for Flexible Behaviour

So the Love Not Smoking: Do Something Different method isn't about giving up. It's about getting back. Getting back your self-control, your health, your money, your relationships and your life. More importantly, though, it doesn't force you to exercise your willpower or change your thinking; it targets your behaviour. In deciding to become a non-smoker you have already decided to change. You want a different future. But flexible behaviour is necessary for change and, unless you do something different, the present will become permanent. We show you how to make the simple changes that are necessary to have more flexible behaviour.

Smokers Are Not Thinner

Many people worry about putting on weight if they stop smoking. More tragically, many people (young women especially) start smoking and continue to smoke in the misguided belief that they have to choose between their health and their figure. As one of our quitters put it, 'I don't think of the extra pounds, I think of all the extra years I'll have in which to lose them.' Yet, look around you and compare smokers and non-smokers. Are the smokers all thinner than the non-smokers? No. Millions of non-smokers manage their weight successfully without smoking. And smokers can do so just as easily.

Do Something Different

The programme in this book and in the accompanying app (www.lovenotsmoking.com) operates on the same Do Something Different principles that we used successfully in The No Diet Diet. So it is just as effective at tackling eating habits as smoking habits. We know from our research that this is an effective approach and one that is in tune with the way the brain's cognitive system works. It actually works with the brain rather than trying to wage war against it, so eating and smoking addictions can both be busted. In fact, research from Northwestern University, published in the scientific journal *Addiction*, found that trying to tackle weight and smoking at the same time actually produced added benefits. The women in their study were able both to stop smoking and control their weight, proving that they didn't need to choose between the two. Because our technique breaks habits that sustain all kinds of maladaptive behaviours, including overeating and smoking, it ensures that when you quit you don't use food as a substitute for cigarettes. Also, because we know the behaviour-optimization aspects of the programme can help combat stress and anxiety, you won't need to comfort eat or to smoke to relieve stress (it's well known that ex-smokers are less stressed than when they smoked), and you'll emerge feeling more fulfilled and with a richer life.

Why Stop in the Name of Love?

By the way, you may be wondering why this book is called *Love Not Smoking*. We chose that title for the book because we are convinced that by the end of it you will love not smoking far more than you thought you loved smoking. But there's another reason. You may have bought this book for yourself, but chances are someone gave it to you. That person bought it for you for one simple reason: because they love you.

And they would prefer it if you didn't smoke. In fact, they desperately want you to give up smoking, for yourself and also for them. In the words of the Supremes (if you're not old enough to remember them, we're talking three sober Amy Winehouses in taffeta frocks here), they want you to 'stop in the name of love'. They may not be able to tell you (or sing it) but they are terrified that one day they'll lose you because of your smoking. By giving you this book they are communicating to you what really, really matters in the world. What's most important. And it's love. Not smoking.

Chapter 2

WHY IT WORKS

If you're impatient to get started on the programme and can't be doing with delving into all the whys and wherefores, that's fine with us. Just butt out here, skip to Chapter 8 and get started. But if you want to know more, read on.

There's no getting away from it: smoking is a compulsive, destructive addiction from which millions of people have struggled to break free. Millions have succeeded, too.

> It's time to stop seeing smoking as just a physical addiction. It is also a behavioural and psychological addiction, one that's hooked up to many other habits that you have.

A whole raft of research has shown that the urge to smoke is actually very 'context-dependent'. That means, strangely enough, that certain situations seem almost to urge and compel you to smoke. So you can't quit easily without tackling all the contexts that spark you off in this way and avoiding those situations where you would usually smoke, or at least altering them in some way. You can't quit without making changes to lots of different things that you do, and to where and how you do them. Many other methods have tried to break the connection between smoking and the trigger cues, but our technique goes further than that. It recognizes that your whole lifestyle is saturated with engrained habits, routines and cycles of behaviour connected to smoking. All kinds of things you do without even thinking about them can cue your smoking. From the moment you get up in the morning and first reach for your cigarettes, to the moment you stub out the last one before bed, your life is a set of smoking triggers. So the Love Not Smoking: Do Something Different technique works by breaking down the whole complicated *web* of habits that support and maintain your smoking. Because everything is connected to everything else. You may have thought you were hooked, but we're going to unhook you.

The Web of Habits

Let us explain further. No doubt you've come across people with a will of iron and steely, rock-solid determination, reduced to gibbering wrecks when it comes to quitting smoking. In fact, four out of five people who try to quit fail. Why? We know it's because they simply didn't dismantle the whole web of habits that was interwoven with their smoking. They tackled smoking as if it was an isolated behaviour in their life, totally disconnected from everything else they do. They tried to summon all their resolve and willpower to overcome the pull of nicotine.

Huge mistake.

As a long-term expert in the dubious art of smoking, you'll know your daily life is jammed full of things that trigger the urge to smoke. A cup of coffee. A stressful meeting. A party. An argument. A drink down the pub. A phone call. Sex. These have fashioned in your brain a powerful link between hundreds of events in your life (both large and small) and the act of having a cigarette. And when one of those events occurs? Whoosh! Your brain automatically sends you down a well-trodden path of past association. And you can bet your last packet that there's a cigarette at the end of that path. Smoking is the final conditioned act at the end of a sequence of predisposing events.

Willpower Is Weak

Willpower alone is weak in the face of this powerful force. Willpower cannot unravel all those links. It can't derail the brain once its unstoppable journey has been set in motion. It's virtually impossible. It struggles to overcome the force of habit. And anyway, there's only so much willpower to go round. We talk about this more in Chapter 4, where we go more into other quit methods. Unless you learn to work around the cues in the environment and trick your brain down another path, your potential to give up smoking will be scuppered. The only way is to start breaking up all those links; to start reprogramming your brain so it doesn't expect an influx of nicotine every time it bumps up against one of those triggers; to jolt it into a network of new connections, patterns and experiences.

The Brain Can Change: Neuroscience Tells Us So

In recent years neuroscientists have learned much about the role of new experiences in the development of the brain. Although you are born with virtually all the brain cells you will ever have, it is your life experiences that determine the strength of the connections formed between certain brain cells. These connections are what accounts for brain growth. And the more the brain is stimulated, the more brain connections it will form, and the more those connections will grow and flourish. In fact, when scientists studied the brains of taxi drivers, whose training requires them to memorize thousands of roadways and routes, their memory part of the brain – the hippocampus – was much larger than that of the average person. More recently, researchers at Oxford University showed that structural changes occurred in the brains of volunteers who were trained to juggle. More and more science is showing us that experience can shape the brain, and extensive rewiring can happen at any stage during adulthood.

It's a two-way process. The brain doesn't just influence what you do. What you do also influences the brain. And the more you do something different, the greater the chance of new brain growth, of breaking away from the old patterns that keep you smoking.

Here's the neuroscientist Gregory Berns' take on this, in his book *The Iconoclast*: 'The brain is lazy. It changes only when it has to. And the conditions that consistently force the brain to rewire itself are when it confronts something novel. Novelty equals learning, and learning means physical rewiring of the brain.'

This turns some of the old ideas about the brain on their head, if you'll pardon the pun. It used to be thought that the brain had designated areas for particular functions. This was a view of the 'localizationalists', and there is a certain amount of truth in this. We do, for example, have a visual cortex devoted to sight, an auditory cortex for hearing and an area devoted to language, called Broca's area. The 'neuroplasticians', however, have also shown that these areas are less fixed than used to be thought, and that the brain can restructure itself. Scientists such as Alvaro Pascual-Leone from Harvard Medical School have demonstrated that the individual parts of the brain are not necessarily committed to processing particular senses. In fact the brain can be reorganized so that different parts perform different tasks, and this can even happen within a matter of days.

The neuroplastic (or malleable) properties of the brain give rise to our potential for flexibility, growth and change – *if* we are willing to exploit it. Pascual-Leone even goes as far as to liken the brain to Play-Doh, so strong is his belief in its ability to be remodelled.

Novel Experiences Create New Connections

This is all good news, because it means you can exploit the neuroscientists' findings and apply them to your own habits and your own lifestyle. Your smoking habits may have become hard-wired into your brain, but that doesn't mean they can't be changed. You just have to create a behaviour that is at odds with the habitual one. The Love Not Smoking: Do Something Different programme breaks down all your old, habitual associations and drops into their place new, different, better associations. Novel and unusual experiences create new pathways and connections. It uses solid, scientific behavioural techniques to subtly reprogramme what you do every day. To get your smoking needs met without using nicotine. And to bombard your brain with things it has never encountered before.

The programme does this in ingenious yet simple ways. As we said, it first breaks up the previously stored connections you had in your brain. Those are the links between what you do and when you smoke. Then it helps you to do things slightly differently so that your brain doesn't associate the new behaviours with smoking. The ability to forge new connections in the brain is limited only by your ability not to go down one pathway and to choose a new one instead.

The tool with which you do this is *action*.

Doing Something Different

As motivational expert Robin Seiger says in his book *42 Days to Wealth, Health and Happiness*, 'Without taking action our hope ends up becoming little more than wishfulness.'

Novel actions and new behaviours are the potent ingredients in the Love Not Smoking: Do Something Different programme. Let's face it, up until now many of your repeated patterns of behaviour have probably sent a message down a brain pathway with a sign at the end of it that says, 'Smoke! Now! Go on, light one up!'

You've virtually wired smoking into your brain's circuitry.

Your smoking has been embedded in a history of past behaviours and conditioning. That's where the reprogramming is going to be targeted: at the plethora of sensory and behavioural cues that have become encoded in your brain's circuitry and leave it gagging for regular doses of nicotine.

Getting Ready to Quit: Easy Does It

Before you even give up (in two or three weeks' time), we'll start preparing you by slowly and gently breaking up some of those old well-connected pathways. We'll show you how to start disrupting the habit web in a diverse set of ways, so that when you come to quit, it will be so much easier. Nothing painful, nothing drastic, just juggling the synapses a bit. You might even have a bit of fun.

You'll start off with making some changes in a space at home (or work or even your car) – any place where you frequently smoke. It will become your first No-Smoking Zone. That starts to tackle one environmental trigger. While still smoking, you'll begin to learn how to split up events that were previously connected. So if you've always had a coffee and a cigarette, you'll still have a coffee and a cigarette. Just not at the same time. This process gradually chips away at the links in the chain of habits that condition you to light up. The Love Not Smoking app will help you to make this change, wherever you are, while you can get help and inspiration at any time from our support group on www.lovenotsmoking.com

'The sex was so good even the neighbours had a cigarette afterwards.'

Pavlov's dogs' brains sent their salivary glands into overdrive on hearing a bell ring before their food appeared. In just the same way, your nicotine receptors have learned to jump up and down with excitement on encountering certain triggers. Not a bell ringing perhaps. But a phone ringing, maybe? The sound of a cork popping? A friend's voice? The gurgle of the coffee machine or the crinkling of the cellophane wrapper on a cigarette packet? This is classic conditioning, one of the brain's most fundamental and rapid learning mechanisms. That's why even humans need a bit of reconditioning now and again.

Heavy or Light, They're All Smokers

We'll introduce other habit-busters and disruptors so gradually that the whole chain of connections and triggers will be weakened. Then you'll quit in the third week of the programme. This approach is important whether you smoke two a day or 50. Anna Mertziani at the University of Hertfordshire carried out research into the habit chains of people who considered themselves 'light' or 'heavy' smokers, and found there was little difference between them. Heavy smokers are defined not just by the number of cigarettes they get through in a day but by how soon after they get up they need to have their first puff. The earlier it is, the stronger the addiction. Even so, people who consider themselves light smokers still have those habit chains, and these condition them to need to smoke in certain contexts.

Life-Changing

People have told us the Love Not Smoking: Do Something Different programme changes their whole life. In nice ways, of course. As one fan put it, 'When you Do Something Different, magic happens.' So don't be taken aback if you get more than you bargained for. It's because the programme bamboozles your network of behaviour patterns in their entirety, even those of which you weren't aware. Another reason is that you start to make conscious choices instead of being on autopilot. You challenge old assumptions and embrace new thinking. When you disorient yourself a bit from your old ways of being, you'll see and experience the world differently. And the programme may shed light on how your habit web has been preventing you from enjoying life to the full. So don't be surprised if you find you sleep better, keep to a healthy weight, your relationships improve or you just have more of a zest for life. But one thing's for certain: you'll find that you love not smoking.

You may have heard the old joke about two old men sitting in a gloomy, dingy old people's home, staring at a fuzzy television and surrounded by snoring geriatrics. One says to the other, 'Just think, if we hadn't given up smoking and drinking we'd have missed all this.' Don't believe that things can't be better than they are. Life can be just as good as you want to make it.

Quitting: You Know It Makes Sense ... But...

First of all, let us ask you something: are you 100 per cent sure that you want to stop smoking? Search deep into your soul for the answer to that question. Because, if you don't, there's little point in you reading any further.

Let's be clear that you must have an absolutely unqualified desire to quit if this is going to work. The more you want to quit, the easier it will be. That also means you need to be willing to put in the effort to quit rather than just fantasizing about it. Don't believe those people who say you just need to visualize something and it will happen. If only it were that easy. Our colleague and friend Professor Richard Wiseman looked at the research on visualization for his book *59 Seconds* and concluded, 'The message from the research is clear – fantasizing about your perfect world may make you feel better but is unlikely to transform your dreams into reality.' Only taking action can turn dreams into reality.

So you know the reasons for quitting and we don't want to labour them. Thankfully, everyone's been brainwashed with the 'smoking kills' message ever since Richard Doll discovered the link between smoking and cancer. That's why you won't find much in this book about *why* you should give up smoking. OK, we guess you're not too fond of the idea that smoking cures salmon but kills people. Or that it gives you smelly breath and bad teeth. Or that it costs you a small fortune and you could spend the money on better stuff. You know all that, of course.

That's not to say there isn't a part of you that would like to hang on to the habit. We suspect you're not too excited about quitting because you think you'll miss it. As one would-be quitter put it, 'I concentrate better with it; I won't be the same person if I don't smoke. What will I do when I'm drinking, around smoking friends, on lunch breaks at work or in the house when I'm watching TV at night?' Deep down, you've been brainwashed into believing you can't do without it. You simply can't imagine life without the pleasure you get from putting a flame to a cigarette and inhaling deeply (never mind that millions of non-smokers get by without that feeling every day of their lives).

Motivation to quit comes from a solid belief that smoking *isn't* something to be missed. If you embark upon a quit-smoking programme expecting to feel the blow of self-deprivation, or crippling self-sacrifice, you'll fail. Accept that the part of you that's daunted by the fear of missing smoking is merely the automatic part of your conditioned brain, pleading. Accept that it's there, but don't give it too much credence. We will show you that you won't miss smoking. In fact, we'll go further than that: we guarantee that you'll love not smoking much, much more than you think you now love smoking.

But I'm Addicted to Nicotine!

'But I'm addicted to nicotine!' we hear you cry. Maybe so but, let's face it, we are not only dealing with a physical dependency here. If we were, you'd be able to slap on a nicotine patch, bin the cigs and say, 'Hello non-smoker.' We go more into the nature of addiction in Chapter 3. When Anna Mertziani from the University of Hertfordshire scrutinized a vast amount of scientific literature on smoking cessation for her doctoral thesis, she concluded that, 'The role of behavioural techniques is crucial for smoking-cessation programmes, as handling the physiological dependence alone is proven to be a weak strategy.' Nicotine dependency is behavioural and psychological as well as physical, and that's why this programme works on your behaviours and your psychology. A nicotine patch alone has a desperately tough job to do if you continue to live the same life, think and do the same things, and expose yourself to all the triggers that cause you to smoke. You may as well try to climb Everest in your flip-flops. But if you really want to quit smoking and get a better life, read on.

Chapter 3

WHAT'S BEHIND THE PROGRAMME? AND CAN IT FIGHT ADDICTION?

Confession Time

OK, dear reader, Ben has just slipped out of the room, so I'm going to let you in on something. I knew that he had once smoked, as a young man at Oxford, and I just asked him why he started. His answer was swift and unhesitating: 'For effect,' he said.

Well, that's honest, I thought. Especially since he smoked a huge Sherlock Holmes-type pipe, so I wondered exactly what kind of 'effect' he was after!

I guess, like most young people, he wanted to look grown-up.

'If no adults smoked,' Ben ventured, 'do you think any kids would take it up?' He's got a point there. Put that in your pipe and smoke it. Or rather, don't.

I thought more about the 'for effect' answer and back to my own early days. When I was about 12, my brother had some friends round for a party. His friends were all around 14 or 15 and, I thought then, the height of coolness. Cool by my standards meant they had acne, the latest Beatles record and a vocabulary of rude words. None so cool, though, as the one who brought along his sophisticated girlfriend. Except, when I looked closer, she was actually Sylvia Mellors, a girl in form 2B, in *my* year at school. There was Sylvia, looking nothing like a schoolgirl but resplendent in make-up, a miniskirt and – god forbid – nylon stockings! I withdrew farther into the corner where I'd been reading my *Bunty* and – clocking those nylons again – tucked my feet under me to hide the regulation school socks that I realized, to my horror, I was wearing.

Then, it happened.

Sylvia Mellors might just as well have taken out a sign that said, 'I am the coolest Miss Cool since cool was invented' (except we probably would have used the word 'groovy' then), because she took from her elegant gold clutch bag ... a CIGARETTE.

My tiny jaw, still fresh from thumb-sucking, must have hit the floor and my pigtails stood on end as I watched, entranced, as her BOYFRIEND (who was a *boyfriend*, I tell you, not a friend who was a boy) leaned over, flicked a lighter and lit her cigarette for her. She inhaled. I could have eaten my bobble hat. I was transfixed. I had just witnessed the most classy act any human being could perform. Yes, you see, I was growing up and my impressionable, naïve, adolescent brain with its identity-seeking sensors was frantically at work.

Nico-teens

It wasn't until a few years later that I accepted a puff of a cigarette from another 'cool' girl at the local youth club, but the 'smoking is hip' message had been firmly imprinted on my brain. And the impression was far, far stronger than any of the anti-smoking messages which were around at the time. Because the main drivers of the adolescent brain are not 'Think of the future, live longer, live healthier.' The adolescent brain is marinated in sex hormones that scream, 'Think of now, appear cool, have an identity, attract a mate and, for goodness' sake, do try to look grown up.'

Having said that, none of us wants our own children to smoke. When adults see young kids smoking in the street, we don't think they're cool. I don't know about you, but they always make me feel a bit sad, particularly the very young ones, who themselves are barely larger than a king size and who'd look more at home with a lollipop in their mouths than a cigarette. In England almost one in ten children aged from 11 to 15 admits to being a regular smoker, and the trend for children to take up smoking continues.

I remember that first puff I took and the first cigarettes I began to sneak in afterwards. The taste was foul. I wanted to throw up. But I suppressed my gagging reflex and, beneath purple-glittered lids, eyed the admiring glances of my mates as I became one of them, one of the in-crowd. The major drivers in adolescence are acceptance by one's peers and outright rejection of anything perceived as old and stodgy. Parents, teachers and governments with their admonishments and advice fall firmly into the latter category. Although the National Health Service is putting huge efforts into mass media and point-of-sale measures to prevent the uptake of smoking by children, they have got their work cut out in trying to counter the incredibly powerful peer role model, or Sylvia Mellors, effect.

> **The teenager tasting a cigarette for the first time is repulsed and often, literally sickened.**
>
> **The adult tasting their two-thousandth cigarette claims it to be sublime.**
>
> **They are experiencing the same cigarette taste.**

The difference is that adults experience relief from an 'addictive' craving (we'll come to what it means to be addicted later). Because all a cigarette does is make you want another one. The child hasn't yet reached that stage, but she or he soon will (and research shows adolescents get hooked easier than adults). Without the craving-relief, you see, cigarettes on their own are not the most pleasurable sensory experience. If they were, the local deli or the pick 'n' mix at the cinema would be awash with nicotine-flavoured snacks or nicotine jelly sweets. Cigarettes aren't tasty because toxins taste disgusting and the manufacturers can only go so far in disguising this. And the poor, deluded, hoodwinked, addicted brain has learned to override this just to get its fix. Sad.

> **In a 2001 Omnibus Survey conducted by the UK's Office for National Statistics, smokers were asked, 'If you had your time again, would you smoke?' A whopping, wheezing 83 per cent of them said, 'No.'**

Fortunately, both Ben and I gave up smoking early on in life. Not so a friend of ours, James, a lawyer who has smoked for 30 years. He claims he's trying to cut down, but is also adamant he doesn't want to stop smoking. 'I love smoking,' he told us recently, 'It gives me so much pleasure. I've got to die of something, so why should I give up?' At that moment a squeal came from the garden as his eight-year-old son caught a ball his friend had thrown. 'So when will you be encouraging Max to start smoking?' I asked. 'What?!' James spluttered. He found the question ludicrous. But it demonstrates that even the most ardent fans of smoking don't truly and honestly believe their own PR. You never hear them say, 'My kids have got to die of something, so why shouldn't they smoke?'

Tobacco Manufacturers Catch Them Young

Combine the impressionability of youth with the vulnerability of adolescents to nicotine addiction and it's particularly alarming that the World Health Organization (WHO) revealed in 2008 that most people start smoking before the age of 18. What's more shocking is that a quarter start using tobacco before the age of ten. Yes, ten. This happens mostly in developing countries where underage smokers are aggressively targeted by tobacco manufacturers. The tobacco giants know the importance of catching them young; and spend billions of dollars on advertising, promotion and sponsorship, primarily to hook young women and to weaken cultural opposition to tobacco use. After all, with so many smokers dying from using tobacco, what else can the manufacturers do but try and entice others to partake?

Women and Smoking

On World No Tobacco Day 2010, the WHO issued this ominous pronouncement: 'Women are a major target of opportunity for the tobacco industry, which needs to recruit new users to replace the nearly half of current users who will die prematurely from tobacco-related diseases.' Recent research from Harvard University in the USA warns that the lung-damaging effects of smoking may be greater for females than for males. And yet the rising prevalence of tobacco use by young girls continues. In the UK, for example, boys and girls under 13 are equally likely to smoke on a regular basis. However, from age 14 girls take the lead, with 14 per cent of girls aged 14, and 25 per cent of girls aged 15, smoking at least once a day (compared with 10 per cent and 16 per cent of boys, respectively). The highest prevalence of smoking is among the 20–24 age group, accounting for more than 1 million young adults in the UK (data from the Information Centre). It's not so different across the Atlantic, either, where a national survey found that in the USA young adults have the highest smoking rate of any age group.

Addiction

So how come people carry on smoking when the costs clearly outweigh the benefits? Why do they get hooked? Because nicotine is a drug and, like many drugs, it is addictive. And the cigarette is an efficient nicotine delivery system. A single puff leads to swift absorption of nicotine into the bloodstream and the rapid transportation of a high concentration 'bolus' of nicotine to the brain by the arterial circulatory system. This stimulates the adrenal glands so the smoker gets a rush of epinephrine (adrenaline). As well as nicotine, thousands of toxic chemicals in tobacco – including arsenic and carbon monoxide, and the carcinogens benzo(a)pyrene, aromatic hydrocarbons and nitrosamines – enter the body. Some of these chemicals are also found in rat poison and the insecticide DDT. Hardly sounds irresistible, does it?

The 'Pleasure' Reward

There's another powerful force at work, too. Nicotine also activates the reward pathways in the brain, releasing the feel-good chemical dopamine. Dopamine fuels the brain's reward system and lies behind all types of addictions, accounting for that buzz or high that many describe. Although its pleasure-giving qualities are undeniable, neuroscientists have recently been discovering that other neurochemical systems and brain circuits also play a role in nicotine addiction. The involvement of the pedunculopontine tegmental nucleus is a primary example; this is a brain region not traditionally linked to the actions of other addictive substances, and scientists are still trying to understand how the many regions of the brain can support a maladaptive habit.

Without a doubt, though, there's a lot of complex neurochemistry going on in the smoker's brain to deliver them a delightful dopamine reward. The effect wears off very quickly, however, so the smoker needs to continue dosing themselves to keep getting the pleasurable effect. Smokers get, on average, 10 hits per cigarette, so a pack-a-day person is getting around 200. And with time they need more and more of the drug to achieve the same level of satisfaction. They are caught in a cyclical, self-destructive pattern of behaviour. Addiction.

Researchers from the National Drug and Alcohol Research Centre at the University of New South Wales define addiction as:

- A strong and sometimes overpowering desire to take alcohol, drugs or tobacco
- Difficulty in controlling use and
- Associated problems due to use

Unlike psychoactive drugs and alcohol, nicotine does not have immediate associated problems or make the users particularly troublesome. Unpleasant to be around, perhaps, and a bit smelly. But smokers don't do stupid things, feel the urge to sing badly, pick fights or come home with a traffic cone on their heads. And even though smoking is being banned in more and more public places, it is still not wildly unacceptable to be seen indulging in the habit. The consequences of smoking are more long term and certainly less embarrassing or socially alienating. Yet, in many ways, they are far, far more devastating to the health of the individual.

The Diagnostic and Statistical Manual of the American Psychiatric Association (DSM-IV), which is used by clinicians to check whether someone has one of the listed illnesses, still classifies nicotine use as a substance disorder. One reason for this is that it has societal, personal and economic impacts. The short-term effects on the individual include increased pulse rate, temporary rise in blood pressure, decreased blood flow to extremities (toes and fingers), increase in stomach acid, nausea and watery eyes. The long-term consequences include a reduction in the sense of smell and taste, premature wrinkling of the facial skin and increased risk of coughs and colds, bronchitis, emphysema, heart disease and certain types of cancer. It's known to kill people early, and many of those who don't die end up being a huge burden on the health service.

The Addictive Personality

Scientists are still debating whether or not some individuals are more prone to addiction than others. There's no simple answer to this question. As to the debate about the existence of the 'addictive personality', well, the jury is still out on that one, too. One thing's for certain, though. Scientists have not been able to discover a disease called 'addiction'. What they do seem to agree on is that addiction stems from an interaction between the individual's genes and his or her environment. It's not all simply down to the way you were born or the way you were brought up. Your biology is not your destiny, nor can you blame it on your parents. Although twin studies have shown that between 40 and 70 per cent of a person's risk for addiction comes from their genes, this merely hints at some people being more susceptible than others. Does that mean addiction is inevitable for those individuals? Are some babies born to grow into addicts as adults? No (even though pregnant smokers have babies who are more likely to smoke in later life), because generally myriad factors in the environment will influence whether a straightforward genetic predisposition gets translated into a reality. And modern science is revealing that genes are not static, so even if we have a gene, it may not be active at the same level all of the time. Scientifically it's a complex picture, but we can rest assured that addiction is not inevitable or unavoidable.

Are Your Genes on Your Side?

So, if some people are at a slight genetic disadvantage when it comes to addiction, are there also some people who will be genetically advantaged when it comes to quitting or even surviving smoking? The National Institute on Drug Abuse (NIDA) in the USA reported on research that is shedding light on the role of genes in the ability to succeed at quitting, as well as people differing in their susceptibility to smoking-related diseases. We've all heard of so-and-so's granny who smoked 80 a day and lived until she was 103 while still playing squash and tap-dancing for England. Many smokers take huge comfort from such cases. But we don't know how much of a genetic anomaly granny was. And just because she outweighed the odds it doesn't mean every other smoker will. In fact, from the statistics on smoking-related deaths, we know they probably won't.

Adolescents, the research has shown, may be more vulnerable than adults to the reinforcing effects of tobacco components, and recent studies have also identified specific genes that may increase the risk of addiction in adolescence. So the early starters are also the ones who go on to be more addicted and more resistant to attempts at quitting.

Is Addiction a Choice?

At this point many smokers will throw up their hands and say they can't give up nicotine because they are physically addicted to it.

> While we accept the biological, physical element of addiction, let's not forget it co-exists with a complex set of social, behavioural and emotional factors.

It's not just biologically stimulating substances to which people get addicted. They also get hooked on non-substance-based behaviours. Like sex and gambling. Running, computer games, porn. Or catastrophically bad TV soap operas. Some scientists, like the Canadian psychologist Bruce K. Alexander, claim there is nothing inherently addictive about so-called addictive substances, and that dependency is not an inevitability. He points out that many thousands of hospital patients every year receive morphine in high doses as a form of pain relief, but leave hospital no more an addict than they were before they checked in.

People Do Stop – Just Like That

Then there's the study of Vietnam war veterans, first published in the *Journal of Epidemiology* in 1974. It highlights how many American soldiers used heroin (an opiate drug) while on duty in Vietnam. For most of these young men it was their very first encounter with drugs. Yet it virtually became a way of life on their tour of duty, a method of coping with the atrocities they encountered. When they were back on home soil, a group of psychiatrists from the University of Washington followed up the soldiers and their drug use. Many of the men had felt they were heavily 'addicted' to opiates during their service in Vietnam. Yet 90 per cent of those heavy addicts simply stopped using heroin once they were back home. They claimed they didn't crave the drug or miss it, and couldn't imagine using it again. A change of environment, a change of habit.

Addiction seems to be largely context-dependent. One woman in our smoking-cessation research, 44-year-old Marion, told us that she had smoked since she was 15 and considered herself a heavy smoker. Yet whenever she dated a non-smoker, she would stop for the duration of the relationship. If she dated a smoker, she would smoke more. Although Marion's answer to quitting would seem as simple as picking a non-smoker, she did admit that her criteria for a potential partner stretched a little further than that!

Rat Cage or Rat Park

Bruce K. Alexander, in his book *Peaceful Measures, Canada's Way Out of the War on Drugs*, describes giving lab-caged rats opiates-on-tap and finding that they shamelessly overindulged themselves. But when he gave the same supply to rats in a friendly, luxurious (by rat standards) 'rat-park', there was none of the said drug-bingeing. These contented rats, who were living fulfilled and happy lives, could take or leave the drug. So this calls into question the very concept of any 'natural' predilection for addictive substances, given the huge variability in depth of 'addiction' according to context.

Rat-cage or rat-park: what kind of environment do you live in?

Beliefs Are Addictive, Too

When our guard is down we can become as addicted to our own ideas as we can to a whole host of substances.

Hang on doggedly to the idea that your addicted body is shackled to a dependency and you increase the likelihood of sabotaging your own attempts to quit. Your own thoughts can create a potent cocktail of self-limiting belief and self-fulfilling prophecy. Mind these words from psychologist Jeffrey A. Schaler in his book *Addiction is a choice*: 'To someone engaged in a bitter struggle to give up one way of life and find a replacement, it is discouraging and demoralizing to be informed that their old way of life is somehow fated, predetermined by their body chemistry.'

Schaler is convinced that involuntary addiction is a myth and that all our conscious actions are under our voluntary control. He points out that everyone who starts to smoke chooses to do so. Very rarely is it forced upon them. If quitters can also choose to stop smoking, as millions have, so can anyone who smokes. And it's not just ideas and beliefs that are the culprits. Schaler also shares our view that habits are what keep people smoking: 'Because all our beliefs, values, habits and physiological responses are an intricately woven web...' That's where change has to be targeted.

Life-Change as Catalyst

We hope we've convinced you that merely treating the physical dependency on nicotine is just one insignificant sub-plot in the quitting story. For some people, a complete change of environment can be the catalyst to beating the addiction for good, like the Vietnam vets coming home. Often a change of job, partner or even country does the trick. Or a new frame of mind. Many women get pregnant and simply quit smoking.

Addicted until that blue line appeared in the pregnancy test window, the prospect of harming their unborn child is enough to make them stop and never start again. The same for people who are diagnosed with a serious health problem. Many leave the physician's consulting room, bin the cigarettes and never look back.

Even the most hardened nicotine 'addict' can resist from smoking when circumstances dictate. A long-haul flight, a no-smoking restaurant or being around a new-born baby forces the urge into the background. Embarrassment or even shame can come into play, too. One smoker, Alison, told us:

I feel kind of embarrassed that I smoke and would hate my nieces and nephews to know that I did. When I'm around them, visiting, I can go a whole day or weekend without even wanting a cigarette. I wouldn't want them to know I smoke (I'm a cool aunty to them and I don't want them to think it's OK) and somehow that translates into not needing it. That lasts until I drop them off/head home!

So, as well as smoking triggers, there can be tangible smoking-inhibitors, too. Knowing what these are, whether people or places, and making a conscious effort to bring more of them into your life can stack the odds of quitting for good in your favour.

Life Goes on Just the Same

Generally, though, most people's lives just aren't that variable. They simply don't have that degree of choice over contexts and circumstances. Some even go so far as to see themselves as victims. When trying to quit smoking, they remain in exactly the same environment and the same frame of mind as they did when they were a smoker. That's where behavioural interventions come in. We can't introduce a seismic shift into someone's life or create the catastrophe that would make them quit. But changing small behaviours can have the effect of making minor disruptions to the current environment when a complete change is out of the question. Behavioural tremors rather than a complete earthquake. According to NIDA's research report on tobacco addiction published in 2009: 'Behavioral interventions play an integral role in smoking-cessation treatment, either in conjunction with medication or alone.'

Behavioural Therapies Are What Works

The NIDA report emphasizes strongly, and we echo their view, that the big tug of addiction, the main force behind it, is a behavioural and psychological one. To quote from their report again:

Although withdrawal is related to the pharmacological effects of nicotine, many behavioral factors can also affect the severity of withdrawal symptoms. For some people, the feel, smell, and sight of a cigarette and the ritual of obtaining, handling, lighting, and smoking the cigarette are all associated with the pleasurable effects of smoking and can make withdrawal or craving worse. Behavioral therapies can help smokers identify environmental triggers of craving so they can employ strategies to prevent or circumvent these symptoms and urges.

Although NIDA are not specific about the strategies that circumvent the symptoms, our research on this is extremely encouraging and we believe Do Something Different to be the answer.

Chapter 4

WHY THIS METHOD AND NOT SOME OTHER ONE?

Isn't There an Easier Way?

There are probably more ways of giving up smoking than there are brands of cigarettes. They all have their merits and their drawbacks. You may have already tried some of these other methods yourself. Many people who want to quit smoking make repeated attempts and lots of them also fail several times over. Little wonder they feel very disillusioned, resigned and wonder if they're hooked for life. Some end up feeling they simply don't have what it takes to give up. The fact is, though, there are all sorts of odds stacked against them. The methods they have tried may have been too narrow, and too much is invested in them; smoking cessation has become medicalized, and most treatments don't address the lifestyle issues that need tackling. We have to admit to being amused by websites that offer smokers a way of giving up along with the message, 'If you fail, don't give up.'

Don't give up giving up seems to be a ubiquitous message, a slogan unlikely to instil huge confidence in the would-be quitter. As Mark Twain is reputed to have said, 'Giving up smoking is easy. I've done it hundreds of times.'

But let's have a quick look at the alternative methods that are around. In this chapter we'll go into the range of non-pharmaceutical methods that are on offer. That means do-it-yourself approaches and more mind-focused methods. We deal with drugs and nicotine substitutes separately in Chapter 5.

Cold Turkey

This is the term used to refer to simply stopping, without any additional aids. It's cheap, quick and you don't need to chew gum or join classes, go into a trance, stick on patches or stick in needles. So far, so good. Many people have stopped successfully like this, but for most (more than 90 per cent of people) the tug of the old habits means they lapse and give in to the craving. A lack of planning has a lot to do with their failure, too. Although with the Love Not Smoking: Do Something Different method we also encourage you to stop altogether, we put in place all the necessary preparatory steps to arm you for the quit first. Then we support you through it afterwards. Quitting smoking has to be a series of carefully planned steps, and different factors affect people at different stages; that's why we offer a six-week programme with a mobile option to make these steps even clearer. Less cold turkey, more nice warm chicken, we like to think.

Cutting Down

This sometimes goes by the name of nicotine tapering or nicotine fading. This is when the smoker switches to a 'lighter' brand and/or each day reduces the number of cigarettes they smoke until they eventually go cold turkey. At least, that's the idea. It's a method that's attractive to smokers because it's less drastic than cold turkey. And the smokers can kid themselves they are giving up, when in fact they are still smoking. Unfortunately, however, there's a good chance they're puffing twice as hard on those so-called light cigarettes and actually may end up having higher levels of carbon monoxide in their body. Low-tar cigarettes, for example, have the same amount of tar in them as regular cigarettes. They simply have a filter that is more dense. So the smoker draws on it harder to get the same nicotine hit. Similarly, menthol brands merely disguise the fact that they contain the same amount of tar, toxins and chemicals as other cigarettes with a minty flavour. They are not any safer. The only 'healthy' cigarette is the unlit, unsmoked one.

Also, like the dieter who cuts out cakes but ends up dreaming about (and eventually bingeing on) doughnuts, the smoker who cuts down starts to attach enormous significance and desirability to each cigarette smoked. The reward factor when it is smoked hits unprecedented heights. So in reality the person who is cutting down is doing all the right things to make themselves *more* hooked on smoking, not less. They are more likely to inhale more deeply, suck harder and smoke more of the fewer cigarettes they smoke. You might have guessed by now that we're not too wowed by this method, with which around two-thirds of people fail. OK, even if they don't quit, some people may get down to ten a day instead of 50 a day, but the health rewards are far, far greater if they cut out those ten as well.

Sure, in the preparation phase of the Love Not Smoking: Do Something Different programme our would-be quitters sometimes start having fewer cigarettes. That's because they have started removing some of the triggers that cue them to smoke. So that cigarette is needed less, not more.

Acupuncture

This is based on traditional Chinese medicine and involves sticking tiny needles into strategic points in the body and leaving them there for up to 30 minutes. It is claimed that the body's natural energy is rebalanced by this process and the smoker can then manage withdrawal symptoms and quit successfully. Two tiny needles are sometimes inserted in the earlobes and the smoker has to twiddle these whenever he or she gets a craving. It is said that after two weeks of twiddling they no longer feel the urge to smoke. Without putting too fine a point on it (sorry), there are people who swear by acupuncture and for whom it works. And there are people who think the twiddling is a load of twaddle and it doesn't work for them. Could there be a placebo effect going on here? In the absence of any randomized-controlled trials proving that this method works, that's still an open question.

To explain what we mean by this we are indebted to Ben Goldacre and his fascinating book *Bad Science*. A fair randomized-controlled trial involves giving some people 'real' acupuncture and others 'sham' acupuncture, either using fake needles or sticking them in random places rather than the correct acupuncture points. The patient doesn't know whether they've had the genuine or the sham treatment. That way their own expectation of success shouldn't play a role in the outcome. When these sorts of trials of acupuncture for back pain were extensively reviewed recently, the real acupuncture made no more difference to the patients than the sham needles did. Other studies claiming that acupuncture does work, unfortunately, don't adopt this rigorous scientific approach. The patient knows whether they are getting the fake or the real needles, and the mind is very powerful. Trials that do compare active acupuncture with sham acupuncture don't find consistent evidence that it increases the number of people who successfully quit smoking. There doesn't at present seem to be enough evidence to dismiss the possibility that active acupuncture is any more effective than placebo.

Nonetheless, there's nothing wrong with someone quitting smoking due to the placebo effect; in fact we're all for that. We just object to people forking out lots of money for treatments that aren't what they purport to be. And although many quitters claim that acupuncture has worked for them, there are also many others who add this to their list of failed attempts.

Cold Laser Therapy

Sometimes known as low-level laser therapy, this is similar to acupuncture but uses laser beams instead of needles. It is claimed to relax the smoker and stimulate endorphin production (the body's natural painkillers), but there is no scientific evidence that it helps people stop smoking.

Hypnosis

If, by now, you are feeling very sleepy, you may be a candidate for hypnosis. The theory behind it goes like this: a hypnotherapist can make you relax and let go of your conscious mind. They can then gain access to your unconscious mind and plant a message there that you do not want to smoke. Or that you will quit. Then you wake up and look at a cigarette as if it's some kind of lethal weapon. Lots of people are attracted to this because it promises a mysterious magic solution into which they don't have to put any effort. They can just pay someone to sort out the problem for them while they have a pleasant nap. A bit like a plumber popping round and unblocking the sink while you're out, they like the idea that the hypnotherapist will nip in, reprogramme their mind and they'll wake up completely cured. Sorry to sound flippant here, but if it were that easy, everyone who wanted to stop smoking would have stopped by now. It clearly does work for some people, but not for all.

Although hypnosis is a harmless technique that helps some people, a lot of people are making money out of it and there is no scientific evidence for its efficacy. A single session costs far more than this book, and people are usually told they need several sessions for it to work. Randomized trials of hypnotherapy for long-term smoking cessation are still rare. A Cochrane Review that considered nine studies was undertaken, with conflicting results. They concluded, 'We have not shown that hypnotherapy has a greater effect on six-month quit than other interventions or no treatment. The effects of hypnotherapy on smoking cessation claimed by uncontrolled studies were not confirmed by analysis of randomized controlled trials.'

We know that we talk about 'reprogramming' your mind with the Love Not Smoking: Do Something Different method. But that claim is based on an abundance of evidence from the field of neuroscience that learned habits are coded in the brain's neural pathways and that new behaviours can create new brain circuitry. But so far we haven't found a way of you doing it without you also having to stay awake.

Counselling: the Motivational Interview

Despite their enthusiasm for their own pharmacological commodities, it's notable that many drug companies also recommend counselling for people who are trying to stop smoking. How can counselling help a person to quit? Understandably, lots of people doubt whether they can quit alone, feel they need support and venture down to their local health clinic or doctor's surgery in search of help from a trained professional. One of the most common styles of counselling currently used in the UK with would-be quitters is the motivational interview, originally designed to help with alcohol abuse but now frequently used with smokers.

Motivational interviewing is usually described as a directive patient-centered counselling technique. The individual has one or more 20-minute sessions in which they are encouraged to explore and resolve their mixed feelings about quitting. The counsellor adopts a non-confrontational, non-judgemental style and tries to guide (i.e. not browbeat) the person toward a sensible decision. There are variants of motivational interviewing techniques and, naturally, counsellors come in all shapes and sizes and with a range of personal qualities, but the method usually involves addressing the following five 'Rs' (based on recommendations from the American Stroke Association and American Heart Association). These explore:

1. Relevance: the individual's personal reasons for quitting
2. Risks: understanding the short- and long-term risks of smoking
3. Rewards: identifying the benefits of stopping smoking
4. Roadblocks: acknowledging the barriers to quitting
5. Repetition: going over these points at each session/meeting.

A Cochrane Review of research into the effects of motivational interviewing, published in 2010, tentatively suggested it could work, but is accompanied by a strong warning. It suggests treating the research results with caution due to huge variation in how the motivational interviewing was delivered and the quality and completeness of the evidence. In other words, they weren't sure they were always comparing like with like. And they found a 'white coat effect', too. The quit rates were three times higher when the patients underwent motivational interviewing with their doctor, rather than with another kind of health worker. So it is possible that it isn't the technique itself that's effective, but the support and attention of somebody with a white coat and a bunch of letters after their name. (Incidentally, just some brief advice from a medically qualified practitioner increases the likelihood of someone becoming a long-term quitter.)

A large scientific review of dozens of random-controlled studies of motivational interviewing for a range of conditions, published in the *British Journal of General Practice* in 2005, also threw up some fascinating findings.

It found that in 75 per cent of the studies motivational interviewing was better than just dishing out traditional advice, for all types of conditions. Given that smokers are probably quite adept at tuning out traditional this-will-kill-you advice, that's hardly surprising. Yet for smokers the figure dropped down to just two-thirds of the studies reviewed. So a third of studies found no positive effects of motivational interviewing for smokers. And what we believe to be the most revealing statement in their review comes when the authors conclude, 'However, the effect of motivational interviewing in some problem areas, for example weight loss and smoking cessation, is primarily brought about through a change in personal habits' (Rubak *et al.*, 2005*). Again and again it seems that recommendations arising from a wide range of smoking-cessation methods converge on the view that *nothing can happen unless habits are tackled*.

Our take on it is that the motivational interview might be a nice way of helping a smoker decide that, yes, it's about time they kicked the nasty habit. It might clarify for them their reasons for quitting and prepare them to give up. And hearing that from a medically qualified person might strengthen their resolve. But that's the first step of the journey and the motivational interview, in our view, focuses too much on the *why* and not enough on the *how* to quit. The person who wants to give up then needs solid, practical and specific help to tackle the behavioural and psychological habits associated with smoking. That help is here, in the form of the Love Not Smoking: Do Something Different programme.

---

* Rubak, S., Sandbaek, A., Lauritzen, T. and Christensen, B., Motivational interviewing: a systematic review and meta-analysis. *British Journal of General Practice*, 55, 305–312.

Cognitive Therapies

Allen Carr

Now, come on, we couldn't write a book about quitting smoking and not mention the guru of giving up, Allen Carr, could we?

Except he wouldn't like that title because 'giving up' was, according to Allen, the wrong way of looking at it. '*Stopping* smoking' would have been his terminology of choice. Carr was a master of the art of reframing, and his books exhort smokers to ditch the deluded mindset that keeps them enslaved to the nicotine master and take on, once and for all, the free mindset of a non-smoker. Right on, Allen.

Since he published his first bestseller *The Easy Way to Stop Smoking,* in 1985, millions of people have bought Allen Carr's books and tried his 'easy way' of quitting. There's no 'method' as such, just pages of persuasion, urging, argument and opinion. Carr doesn't use scare tactics but he does go to work, in a pretty heavy-duty way, on the smoker's psychology. His compelling, even evangelical, style of writing challenges and disputes the smoker's mindset at every turn of the page. He demolishes the smoker's reasons for smoking, fires up their anger and motivation to quit and relentlessly exposes their justifications as deluded and pathetic. Although some find Carr's style overbearing, he certainly takes no prisoners with his almost hypnotic suggestions that:

- There are absolutely no good reasons for smoking, ever, so smokers are deluding themselves.
- There is nothing to 'give up' and only gains to be had.

- Cigarettes are filthy and disgusting, not enjoyable.
- Nicotine addiction and brainwashing are the reasons people smoke.
- Withdrawal pangs are extremely mild.
- It is never too late to stop.
- The smoker is merely trying to get back the sense of tranquillity and calm that the non-smoker feels all the time.
- Cigarettes don't fill a void, they create it.
- Smokers kid themselves about the risks to their health.
- All smokers have to lie to themselves and other people in a vain attempt to justify their stupidity.

Allen Carr describes how he went from smoking 100 a day to zero (ironically after having hypnosis), with barely a withdrawal pang. His message, which comes through loud and clear in his books, is that it is easy to stop smoking. However, people make it harder for themselves by moping about it and wallowing in indecision. Carr's frame of mind is one that proclaims very loudly, 'Isn't it marvellous that I'm a non-smoker? Rejoice!' What a sad irony it is that he died of lung cancer in November 2006.

With almost religious-like fervour, Carr repeats and repeats one message throughout his books: giving up smoking is easy. He brushes aside the notion that withdrawal symptoms, which he describes as an empty, insecure feeling arising from the lack of nicotine, are a problem. But he does admit that it's the psychological trigger of certain events with which the quitter struggles most. We certainly agree with him there, as he admits, *'Even under my method, responding to triggers is the most common failing.'*

As with all the other methods we've reviewed so far, habits or triggers are the sticking point.

Carr's way to deal with triggers – because he was obviously a perceptive man with keen powers of intellectual reasoning – was to *reason* his way out of them. To apply logic, think his way around the problem and come up with some watertight counter-arguments. In response to the smoke-after-a-meal trigger, he contends:

> *Cigarettes do not make meals or social occasions, they ruin them ... the smokers at that meal are not smoking because they are enjoying the cigarette. They are smoking because they have got to. They are drug addicts. They cannot enjoy the meal or life without it.*

Who could fault his arguments or his logic, or question a man who has been there and done it, and helped many others through the process, too? Reading his book, one isn't surprised that people have been persuaded to quit by Allen. If I were a smoker he would leave me in no doubt that I was indulging in the most stupid, degrading and disgusting activity known to man, and I'd be cringing with shame and questioning my own sanity within a few pages.

That's what Carr had an immense talent for: making people think. His method involves taking the mindset of the smoker and bulldozing it into a shift of gigantic proportions. He convinces the smoker that their thinking is flawed, irrational and stupid, and he doesn't give up until they think differently.

'THINK OF THE WHOLE BUSINESS OF STOPPING AS AN EXCITING GAME,' he booms.

'THINK OF THE NICOTINE MONSTER AS A SORT OF TAPEWORM INSIDE YOUR STOMACH,' he roars.

'THINK HOW MUCH BETTER IT WILL BE WHEN THE LITTLE MONSTER HAS LEFT YOUR BODY, TOGETHER WITH ALL THAT POISON,' he barks.

Think. Think. Think. His arguments are compelling. His logic is flawless. Who could possibly question Allen Carr's rock-solid reasoning? He could have called his book *Think Something Different*.

> But not everyone can think themselves different. Thinking can't always turn off the urge to do what we've always done. Our minds are often powerless and even redundant in the face of automatic, conditioned behaviours. Sometimes it's just easier to *do* something different than to *think* something different.

Not only that; there are now findings from neuroscience research that weren't around when Allen Carr was writing. We know a lot more about how the thinking (cognitive) processes in the brain operate in relation to the doing (motor) processes. These even suggest that by the time we think, it's too late – because we've already decided to act.

The Problem with Thinking

Recent brain research has dished up some pretty amazing revelations about human thinking in relation to human action. Imagine that you decide to tap your finger on the table in front of you. You send a message to your finger to tap. And, obligingly, lo and behold your finger taps. Your thought caused the action. Or did it? In 1985 a scientist called Benjamin Libet studied the brains of people carrying out simple commands, such as finger tapping. He noticed that before the volunteers *thought* of moving their finger, he was able to detect corresponding electrical responses in the brain. In short, Libet was able to predict the exact time of the person's decision to move their finger, a fraction of a second *before* they had made up their mind to do so.

More recently, in 2008, a bunch of clever neuroscientists, including some from the Max Planck Institute for Human Cognitive and Brain Sciences in Leipzig, Germany, published a paper in the journal *Nature Neuroscience* that staggered the scientific community. Like Libet, they had shown that before we are aware that we have decided to do something, our unconscious mind has already registered that intention. But they showed it has done so *up to ten seconds* before. They have even gone on to identify the involvement of different regions of the brain at different stages of the decision-making process, using functional magnetic resonance imaging. Under conditions of free choice, they confirmed that our unconscious mind is making decisions for us long before those decisions even flicker upon our awareness. So when we think we've made a conscious decision to do something at a specific moment, that's an illusion. Counter-intuitive as it seems, our brain knows our decisions before we do.

Without losing ourselves totally in the fascinating but undoubtedly complex world of neuroscience, or getting totally intoxicated by the brain's neurochemistry, we mention this research because it provides food for thought for smokers. It gives us an important clue to how the decision to have a cigarette is made behind the scenes, before the smoker is consciously aware of the desire. That's why no amount of appealing to logic or rationalization of decisions is going to make any difference. Many quitting techniques like those of Allen Carr appeal to the logical, conscious part of the brain. But the conscious part of the brain arrives too late at the scene of the crime to be of any help. Modern brain research shows it's at the *un*conscious, *un*thinking level that most of the dirty work is done. And that's where change has to be targeted.

So Is the Answer NOT to Think?

If cognitively reframing your thoughts doesn't do it for every quitter, and conscious thoughts are victims of their own tardiness, perhaps the answer is to try not to think? Thought-suppression is a topic much loved by psychologists who, thanks to the American psychologist Daniel Wegner, became fascinated by the fact that if you tell someone *not* to think of a white bear, that pesky furry creature pops straight into their head and refuses to leave. Dr James Erskine from St George's, University of London, and Dr George Georgiou from the University of Hertfordshire looked at what happens to smokers when you ask them *not* to think about smoking. They got smokers to do this thought-suppressing for a whole week. Then they compared them with a group of smokers who'd been allowed to give their thoughts about smoking a free rein. They also had a control group who were just told to go about their normal thinking lives. The smoking-suppressors did smoke less during the week they were trying not to think about smoking. But what happened when the experimental week was over? Not only did they revert back to their normal pattern of smoking, they smoked *more* than ever before. In their 2010 paper published in *Psychological Science* the psychologists referred to this phenomenon as 'behavioural rebound'. They concluded that, 'Thought suppression may be more harmful than previously believed.' Not only is it hard to keep a good thought down, but when it reappears it will be imbued with a new found potency.

You Can Think about Doing Something Different – and Do It

It might appear that the upshot to this thinking research is that we have no free will or, if our mind isn't under our conscious control, that we're going to be the victim forever of unwanted thoughts. Let's not forget that much of the research we've just mentioned is really concerned with what happens in the moment. Brain-imagers can only study on-line thinking. You, as a human being, can still think about the future and take a strategic decision to make it different. You can decide to make changes in your life and put things in place to increase the chances of them happening. And don't worry, your brain will come along for the ride. As the author Daniel Pink says, in his book *Drive*: 'We're born to be players, not pawns. We're meant to be autonomous individuals, not individual automatons.'

'Players, not pawns' is an expression we like because it is exactly what Do Something Different is about.

Be a player, not a pawn, in the no-smoking game.

Government Smoking-Cessation Support: UK

A box of goodies popped through our letter box the other day. It was from the UK's National Health Service no-smoking programme. The strong brown box was labelled 'Quit Kit' and inside were stickers, leaflets, charts and even a blue-striped twiddly toy – all designed in the name of quitting smoking. Here is a list of the contents:

1. A leaflet urging us to download stress-busting MP3s
2. A fancy wheel chart for calculating how much we'd save by quitting, depending on how many cigarettes a day are smoked
3. Another leaflet on smoking-cessation medicines available from our local NHS Stop Smoking Service
4. A leaflet with brightly coloured images of boxing gloves, a pressure gauge and a target, and with very brief information on triggers and cravings
5. A large card with a 'Well Done' message on the front and a card inside with the helpline number on it
6. A large Quit Plan sheet with daily reminders and motivators
7. Two sheets of stickers including rainbows, suns, coins and fluffy clouds
8. A plastic 'tangle', 'to keep your hands busy and take your mind off cigarettes
9. Another leaflet with questions to test how much 'willpower' we have.

First, let us say, we wholeheartedly applaud the efforts of the NHS to help people quit smoking. Millions of

pounds have been poured into smoking-cessation initiatives for many, many years. However, it saddens us
to see this use of a scatter approach, the wasted efforts
and funding, and the blatant failure to take account of
research into the subtleties of behaviour change. But,
without fail, the part of the Quit Kit that depressed us
most was the 'willpower checker'. This quiz comprised
a number of questions about the strength of a person's
willpower. After filling it in, a person checks their score.
Someone scoring low is told their willpower needs to
be strengthened. They simply haven't got enough willpower. **Boost your willpower** is one of the headlines in
the leaflet. This is followed by some exercises which,
apparently, will help you to boost your flagging and
woefully inadequate willpower. These involve:

* In Exercise 1: *visualization* ('Imagine yourself as a
  non-smoker')
* In Exercise 2: *thinking* ('Think of a time when you
  achieved something you never thought you could')
* In Exercise 3: *more thinking* ('Think about the
  times when you need a cigarette; think about how
  it feels. This is a craving. Don't fight it, just watch
  it...')

Reams of scientific papers have attested to the weakness of willpower and the fact that it is a limited
resource that is easily depleted and unsustainable.
That's why the programme in this book focuses on
behaviour change, on *doing* something different rather
than thinking something different. It's easier to change
what you do than change what you think. Yet the NHS
seems to want to hammer home the message that you
need *willpower* to quit. And if you haven't got enough,

you need to get *more* (BOOST IT) if you are to quit successfully. The NHS website (www.nhs.uk/smokefree) has lots of quirky widgets and gadgets, and no shortage of information on nicotine replacement and where to go for support. But it offers few pointers to help people do what really matters: *change their behaviour*. Feeling rather saddened by this, and disappointed in the NHS, we packed our Quit Kit off to the local GP surgery and turned to the US programmes for quitting, to see if they have come up with anything better.

Government Smoking-Cessation Support: USA

God bless America, as they say. In the USA there is a National Institutes of Health-sponsored Smokefree campaign (http://smokefree.gov), with which we must say we're pretty impressed. We've only viewed their online offerings (not wishing to squander their resources, even in the name of research) but this certainly offers lots of behavioural advice to quitters in a nicely structured framework, called **START**. START stands for:

S= Set a quit date.
T= Tell your family and friends.
A= Anticipate and plan for the challenges ahead.
R= Remove cigarettes and tobacco products from your home, car and work.
T= Talk to your doctor about getting help to quit.

Lots of the advice in the US programme is practical, with suggestions for different actions to take. It doesn't lecture you or tell you what to think. It hardly even mentions willpower. It tells you what you might like to *do*. For example, there is advice on what to do *instead* of smoking in lots of different situations, such as:

- After meals (*try getting up from the table, brushing and flossing your teeth, and taking a walk*)
- While driving (*try listening to a new radio station, taking a different route, or going by train, carpool, or bus, if possible*)
- While drinking coffee (*try switching to water, juice, or tea. Or change the time you drink your coffee*)
- At a party (*try standing with non-smokers and keeping your hands busy*)

The US Smokefree campaign booklet *Clearing the Air* sensibly says, 'Create some new habits and mix up your daily routine.' Music to our ears! They stress the fact that 'Lifestyle Modification' is absolutely critical to any cessation attempt. In their *Forever Free* booklet, produced in association with the National Cancer Institute and the American Cancer Society, there are pages and pages of *positive addictions*. These are described as activities that you *choose* to do and that you can spend an hour of each day enjoying. There's tons of emphasis on filling the gap that smoking leaves in a person's life with things that have physical, mental or spiritual value. They even have pages and pages of ideas of things to do, from meeting someone new to being with animals to fixing things. And they urge people to harness the power of changing routines and doing something different, particularly in order to avoid temptation. For example, they advise: *stay away from things that you connect with smoking. Do it today and for the next few weeks. These may include:*

- *Watching your favorite TV show*
- *Sitting in your favorite chair*
- *Having a drink before dinner*

What a great START to quitting this gives smokers in the USA. If they can add to it the more detailed, structured programme that is found here in this book, we are optimistic about seeing a huge rise in the numbers of American non-smokers.

Internet and Workplace Support

If you have internet access, don't forget that there are support groups (such as Nicotine Anonymous) and forums out there that can connect you with other quitters. One of the largest is Quitnet.org. Many people find this sort of support invaluable, particularly for sharing tips, getting moral support and staying motivated. Knowing you're not alone, getting encouragement from others, chatting to those who've been through what you're going through can all do wonders when it comes to bolstering your endeavour and determination. But do remember that talking and sharing are never substitutes for changing what you do and taking action.

The Love Not Smoking Facebook support group will give you motivation from fellow quitters and regular advice and inspiration from us. Join today via www.lovenotsmoking.com.

Increasingly, many workplaces offer help for workers who want to quit smoking. Some run smoking-cessation clinics on-site, or support on the job. Others will even pay for employees to attend outside programmes. Find out about what initiatives your employers support.

Helplines

There are also, of course, national helplines with live telephone support. In the USA the number to call is 1-800-784-8669. In the UK it is 0800 121 4637.

Chapter 5

WHY NOT DRUGS OR SUBSTITUTES?

In 1986, the American Cancer Society reported that: 'Over 90 per cent of the estimated 37 million people who have stopped smoking in this country since the Surgeon General's first report linking smoking to cancer have done so unaided.' Nonetheless, a huge industry manufacturing smoking-cessation products has shot up and worked hard to persuade the public that the quitting process requires a stop by the pharmacist's counter instead of the tobacconist's. There is certainly a wide range of products on offer. In this chapter we give you the low-down on their effects, good and bad, and their potential efficacy. However, let's not forget that *most people quit without any added help: no drugs, no patches, no substitutes.* We point this out because it is a fact often drowned out by all the shouting that the pharmaceutical companies do. A scientifically robust and broad-reaching review by scientists Chapman and MacKenzie from the School of Public Health at the University of Sydney, published in 2010, analyzed 662 studies of smoking cessation and revealed the following:

- Two-thirds to three-quarters of ex-smokers give up smoking without any extra help.

- The increasing medicalization of smoking cessation distorts people's perception of what is needed to quit, and attempts to convince them that cessation has to be pharmacologically or professionally mediated.
- Much of the research into assisted smoking cessation, but few, if any, studies into unassisted cessation, are funded by the pharmaceutical companies that manufacture cessation products.

Their report concludes with a number of messages about smoking cessation that they believe should be conveyed to smokers, one of which states: 'A serious attempt at stopping need not involve using NRT [nicotine replacement therapy] or other drugs or getting professional support.' So the good news is that after buying this book you probably don't need to spend any more money on smoking-cessation products. Nonetheless, we still feel we owe readers some information about what these products are and what they do, so here goes.

Nicotine Replacement Therapy (NRT)

When the pharmaceutical industry first released synthetic nicotine products onto the market, they must have been rubbing their hands with glee. It certainly sounded promising to be able to sell addicts a small, safe dose of nicotine, uncontaminated by toxins, chemicals or carbon monoxide and without any of the harmful effects that come from inhaling. And to some extent their enthusiasm has been rewarded with positive findings from studies into the effects of these products (despite a huge bias generally toward studies on assisted, rather than unassisted, smoking-cessation interventions). These products are also heavily adver-tised, and research has shown that the consumer is three times more likely to be confronted by ads for NRT than messages for other methods. The profits of the NRT-manufacturing companies must be catching up with those of the tobacco industry.

Nicotine replacement products come in the form of patches, gum, lozenges, microtabs and inhalers avail-able to buy over the counter. In the UK these products may also be obtainable on prescription. No one prod-uct seems to be appreciably better than the others; it's simply down to personal preference. However, some do deliver nicotine to the body faster than others, with patches being the slowest delivery method. While you are trying to give up, the product delivers a regu-lar dose of nicotine to your body. A Cochrane Review undertaken in 1996 and updated in 2007 examined the effectiveness of NRT compared to placebo and found NRT increased the chances of quitting by between 50 and 70 per cent. The Australian researchers Chapman and MacKenzie point out, however, that these effects may be inflated by giving participants free drugs, which may motivate them to quit to 'please' the researchers, plus the attention that's paid to them itself may bring about a change in their behaviour. It's what psycholo-gists call the 'Hawthorne Effect' and is supported by a Cochrane finding that 51 per cent of industry-funded trials reported positive cessation effects but only 22 per cent of non-industry trials did. Nonetheless, here is a selection of what the industry has on offer to the consumer.

Nicotine Patches

These are like sticking plasters and are applied to dry, hairless skin on your body or upper arm. The location of the patch on your body should be changed every day (and do take off the old one or you'll end up looking like a leopard). They usually come in three strengths and can last either 16 or 24 hours. The 24-hour formulations are more likely to cause sleep disturbance. Some people swear by them; others say they have no effect at all. One of our quitters commented that sticking the patch over her mouth would have helped more, but we can't comment on that.

Nicotine Gum

This comes in a range of flavours and two strengths. It isn't chewed constantly like ordinary gum, but chewed until the flavour has gone and then kept in the mouth between the cheek and the gum. This area has a rich blood supply and so can pick up the nicotine from the gum. Once you feel an urge to smoke, you chew on the gum and then park it again, and so on. Some people get through a lot of gum using this method, as each piece is really only effective for around half an hour.

Nicotine Sprays

Sprays deliver a higher dose of nicotine via the nostrils, higher than other forms of NRT (though still not as much as you get from a cigarette). Users are advised to have no more than 64 sprays a day. It is said to remove the nicotine craving, though sometimes also to irritate the nasal cavities.

Nicotine Inhalators

These come with nicotine-impregnated cartridges that

you load into the inhaler and inhale whenever you get the urge to smoke. Each cartridge has a life of about 20 minutes and people generally need around six a day. Because this method is a bit more fiddly than simply chewing or inhaling, it also occupies the hands, which some people find an added advantage.

Nicotine Microtabs

You pop these into your mouth (not to be swallowed) and keep them under the tongue where they deliver nicotine slowly into the bloodstream. One or two an hour are used, up to a maximum of 40 a day. Some people experience oral irritation from using them but this can be avoided by keeping them in a different location in the mouth each time.

Nicotine Lozenges

These are also taken orally but have the effect of slowly dissolving in the mouth over the course of about half an hour. They come in two strengths and one or two an hour can be taken, up to a maximum of 15 a day. Again, the location in the mouth where they are placed should be varied to avoid irritation, although some people find they experience stomach upset or indigestion after repeated use.

> Interestingly, much of the marketing material for nicotine replacement therapy stresses that the nicotine substitute deals only with the physical addiction. Most products carry a heavy reminder that the behavioural addiction can continue to be a problem. Looks like those old habits are rearing their heads again.

We quote from one popular stop-smoking website:

> As the physical withdrawal symptoms are being
> dealt with, with the aid of the nicotine replacement
> therapy product, this will enable the smoker to
> concentrate on breaking his behavioural addiction
> to nicotine. For the best chance of success in giving
> up smoking, you must look at not only overcoming
> the physical withdrawal symptoms but also the
> situations that trigger the desire to smoke. Even
> though smokers are physically addicted to nicotine
> and when they stop smoking they suffer physical
> withdrawal symptoms, they usually get cravings
> to smoke when they find themselves in certain
> situations that they have always associated with
> smoking. These situations are habitual and the brain
> automatically alerts the smoker that it is time to
> smoke a cigarette at these times.

So it seems the NRT message is that NRT will take care of the nicotine addiction, but beware of the cravings that result from behavioural addiction. We seem to still have a problem here. The manufacturers admit that nicotine replacement therapy doesn't do anything about all those habitual situations or automatic brain processes that urge a person to smoke. Love Not Smoking: Do Something Different does that.

> The research on the success of nicotine replacement therapy shows that for some people it works best when combined with skilled advice and support, but even then cessation rates rarely get above 25 per cent. That still leaves three out of every four people hooked on the habit. And more people quitting without NRT than with it.

If you feel you need nicotine replacement therapy while you are on the Love Not Smoking: Do Something Different programme, then please go ahead, although lots of people have managed with this programme alone. Just remember that if you are on nicotine replacement therapy you must not smoke at the same time, as that can be dangerous and may lead to a nicotine overdose. These are controlled medicines and you really must follow the manufacturers' instructions for safe use. Having said that, many people worry about the side effects listed on the NRT product packs – even though the side effects from smoking are far more dangerous. If you are in any doubt at all, are pregnant or have a specific health condition, then consult your doctor before going ahead. NRT is generally safe for people with diabetes or high blood pressure. Most people start with a high dose and then gradually reduce to a weaker one, and a course of treatment usually lasts three months and should never be undertaken for more than six months. The more you smoke, the manufacturers claim, the heavier a dose you may need.

Don't even think of bothering with herbal cigarettes; they're about as much use as a chocolate teapot. The same goes for herbal dietary supplements that claim to curb nicotine cravings. There is no evidence that these work in spite of what they say on the tin.

Nicobrevin
This is another product sold as an aid to smoking cessation, but so far there have been no scientific studies to establish its effects on long-term smoking cessation.

Anxiolytics
Anxiolytics are drugs that are prescribed to reduce anxiety but, again, with these there is no strong evidence to show an effect on quitting smoking.

Antidepressants

These are medications prescribed to treat depression and there is some evidence that the 'older' types of tricyclic antidepressant (e.g. nortriptyline) increase quit rates. Bupropion also has some success and is now marketed as a smoking-cessation aid, under the name of Zyban (see opposite). There are no studies showing that antidepressants that fall into the category of selective serotonin reuptake inhibitors (e.g. fluoxetine or Prozac) help with smoking cessation.

Clonodine

Clonodine (also known as Catapres) is a prescription drug used to lower blood pressure, and some people have found it lessens the withdrawal symptoms from giving up alcohol or smoking. But the evidence for it upping the number of people able to quit smoking is rather weak, and the FDA in the USA has not approved its use for smoking cessation.

Lobeline

Lobeline is derived from the leaves of a tobacco plant found in India and is an alkaloid from which several commercial smoking remedies have been produced. There is no scientific evidence to indicate it can help people stop smoking, and the side effects can be particularly unpleasant.

Pharmacological Treatments: Drugs Specifically for Giving up Smoking

There are some drug treatments (available in the UK from your GP) that are non-nicotine based. One of these, Zyban, has been around for many years, and another, Champix (or Chantix in the USA), is a more recent arrival, having been licensed in the UK and the USA in 2006.

Zyban

Zyban is the commercial name for the drug *bupropion hydrochloride*. It is not known exactly how Zyban works, as it was developed as an antidepressant drug but was found incidentally to reduce the urge to smoke. However, it is likely that it interrupts the brain receptors linked to the feeling of pleasure that the smoker gets. When it was first introduced into the UK there were a lot of scare stories in the press claiming that people had died from using Zyban. Needless to say, the deaths were very few in comparison to the hundreds who die every day from smoking and whose deaths go unreported by the press. On further investigation most of the deaths were found to be smoking-related and not directly linked to the use of the drug. Or the victims had contraindications and shouldn't have been using Zyban. Because, as with most medicines, it doesn't suit everyone. For example, if you suffer from epilepsy, an eating disorder or liver disease; are pregnant, breastfeeding or under 18, you will not be able to take Zyban.

Once again, this isn't a wonder drug. You can't pop a pill that immediately transforms you into a non-smoker. But, alongside the Love Not Smoking: Do Something Different programme, it might help you to quit and that may also make any side effects (nausea, dry mouth, agitation or sleeplessness) worth putting up with for a while. It can be used alongside nicotine replacement products, too.

The UK Department of Health stated in a letter to smoking-cessation co-ordinators in June 2000 that Zyban was 'indicated as an aid to smoking cessation in combination with motivational support'. So there was no suggestion that the drug alone would be enough to help someone quit smoking. Furthermore, the drug's manufacturers claim that Zyban should only be prescribed to people who are motivated to quit smoking, *and* they say it should be used in conjunction with counselling and support.

Champix

This is the name by which the drug *varenicline* goes in the UK; in the USA it is sold under the trade name Chantix. It has a different mechanism for action to other medications that help smoking cessation. Again, this mechanism isn't fully specified, but it is thought to work by weakening the urge to smoke and countering withdrawal symptoms. Also, smoking while taking Champix is said to be less pleasurable. Clinical trials have shown it works better than Zyban or placebo treatment, with cessation rates in clinical trials of around 44 per cent. But again, it doesn't appear to work on its own. All the participants in the trials also received weekly support, and the UK's National Institute for Health and Clinical Excellence (NICE) guidance recommends it should only be prescribed as part of a programme of behavioural support. This drug hasn't been around for long enough to determine its long-term safety, but no serious adverse side effects have been noted. It does make some people feel nauseous (taking it with a glass of water helps) or have sleep disturbance and abnormal dreams (taking the pill with an evening meal lessens this likelihood). About 10 per cent of people give up taking the drug because they can't tolerate these side effects. Again, it can't be prescribed to under-18s, pregnant or breast-feeding women, or those with severe kidney problems (varenicline is excreted almost entirely by the kidneys).

At the time of writing the safety of taking both Zyban and Champix together, or one of them with nicotine replacement therapy, hasn't been tested – but, given the potency of these medications, combination therapy should only be undertaken with medical advice.

So, Do We Say No to Drugs?

While the drug manufacturers are very keen to sing the praises of these smoking-cessation drugs, it is important to recognize their potential but not to get overexcited about success claims. Most of the positive claims do come from clinical trials, and we're all in favour of the application of science. But there is a note of caution. Think about the type of person who volunteers to take part in a trial of new non-smoking drugs. They are probably highly motivated to quit smoking, and it's well known that motivation is a huge factor for predicting success at quitting. These drug-testers also have to be physically and mentally in good health to take part in a drugs trial. So people with current or even recent depression are ruled out (the action of the drug may be different for patients with some mental health problems) and people with other medical illnesses are also, naturally, excluded from the trials. That means the participants are quite a select bunch. These healthy and keen patients also received behavioural counselling or support as well as the drug. In fact, in the case of the main outcome trial of varenicline, they also went through *12 weeks* of individual counselling. As scientists we can't help wonder why they didn't trial the drug without this support, to be better able to determine its efficacy unclouded by confounding variables. But through the smoke-cloud of clinical research findings, one fact does emerge with crystal clarity: many would-be non-smokers find drugs alone aren't the answer, and behavioural change is a necessary and potent ingredient in any attempt to quit smoking.

The Global Research Neglect of Unassisted Smoking Cessation

This is the title of Chapman and MacKenzie's review paper in which they conclude:

> *The persistence of unassisted smoking cessation as the most common way that most smokers have succeeded in quitting is an unequivocally positive message that, far from being suppressed or ignored, should be openly embraced by primary health care workers and public health authorities.*

Chapter 6

HELPING SOMEONE QUIT

What can the partner, friend or supporter of the would-be quitter do to help them to quit? If you've bought someone this book to help them quit, then you've already taken the first positive step and sent absolutely the right message. You've said, 'I care about you enough to want you not to smoke.' There are still other ways in which you can be an aid, rather than an enemy, as you stand by and watch someone close to you try to quit. After all, you want them to use this book and not end up throwing it at you, so here are a few pointers to help you both get the most from it.

RULE NO. 1 FOR SUPPORTING A QUITTER:
Positive Encouragement

Positive encouragement is the opposite of nagging. Praise the person for wanting to quit. Don't nag them because they smoke, have failed before or taken ages to get round to giving up. Nagging will have the opposite effect to the one you want; it's counter-productive and may even set up a pig-headed deter-mination to carry on smoking. Reminding the quitter of how well they are doing and praising their efforts will smooth the way enormously. Even if they complain about how tough they're finding it, just gently remind them that this is a really positive undertaking, one of the most life-enhancing journeys they have ever taken, and stress how much you admire them for it.

Remind the person who's trying to quit that, however bad they are feeling at any given moment, it won't last for long. And the longer they go without smoking, the sooner they will start to feel better. Singing their praises to other people and showing how proud you are of them will also really bolster their confidence. Don't phrase it negatively ('Jim's a bit of a pain at the moment; he's giving up his beloved cigs ... again!') but become his most ardent fan and advertise his success ('This is Jim's fourth day without cigarettes! Hasn't he done fantastically well? I'm so proud of him!'). Give the other person the confidence to quit one day at a time. If your partner does slip, don't berate them. Treat it as a small setback and help them to get back on track.

Never forget the persuasive power of love. Hugs and kisses can be enormously encouraging. Show with affection how attractive and desirable you find your partner's new smoke-free body, and what a joy it is kissing them. Offer to give them a soothing massage when stress levels get high and they'd normally reach for a cigarette. Who would want to go back to smoking once they discover the love life of a non-smoker is infinitely more passionate?!

Just a minor note of caution, though. Don't be too overbearing with your praise and support, or smother them. Laying it on too thick might be perceived as a pressure that's too hard to take. It's worth checking with the other person whether they want you to ask them every day how they're getting on. And go steady on the advice, too – it's better to ask how you can help than to preach a sermon or become an annoying expert! If you feel they may need extra advice, show them www.lovenotsmoking.com

- Do say: good for you, keep at it, you can do it!
- Don't say: *how* many times have you tried to give up?

RULE NO. 2:
Selfless Motivation

Although it's highly likely that the smoker has other people in mind when they draw up a list of reasons for quitting, ultimately the quitter has to do it for themselves alone. However desperately you would like the other person to quit, they are the one in charge.

If the quitter makes other people the sole reason for quitting, they are likely to fail. So step back from the 'do it for me' and 'do it for the kids' messages. Selfish motivation is powerful and has to come before doing it for others. In relationships, if one person quits solely for the other person, there's a danger that smoking becomes a weapon in the relationship. So if a couple has a row, for example, or one is upset by something the other has done, the quitter may go back to smoking merely out of spite, frustration or disappointment. Similarly, doing it for the kids is fine so long as when the kids are driving everyone crazy and being selfish (as all kids can be) the smoker doesn't think 'to hell with this' and reach for a cigarette. Having said that, kids can put powerful pressure on parents not to smoke and, since no parent wants their child to smoke, the prospect of being a non-smoking role model is one to which most parents would aspire. Because the children of smokers are more likely to become smokers themselves. Besides which, who would willingly want to expose their children or spouse to second-hand smoke and fumes?

Doing it for oneself, for social, financial and health reasons is powerfully motivating, and knowing that others will benefit too is really the icing on the cake. Giving up because you are pregnant is, of course, one of those exceptional situations where the needs of another may come before your own. Knowing the risks of cigarette smoke to the unborn child (low birthweight and increased susceptibility to illness, Sudden Infant Death Syndrome and learning problems) must rank among the highest selfless reasons for not smoking.

And we're not underestimating the power of rewards and incentives here. If quitting for a good cause will spur your loved one on, go for it. Help them set up their own fundraising page at www.justgiving.com and invite others to sponsor the quit.

- Do say: do it for yourself; you are the one who matters here.
- Don't say: think about me/the kids/other people.

RULE NO. 3:
Minimize Temptation

If you're living with someone who's trying to give up then it goes without saying that this isn't the time to throw wild parties and invite your heavy smoking friends round for an all-night boozing session. You may even need to forego some social activities for a while and avoid those places where you know the quitter is likely to be exposed to temptation. Be prepared to swap some of your usual activities together for new ones that aren't associated with smoking. Suggest a walk or the cinema instead of the pub, for example. Arrange an evening of grazing on small snacks or tapas instead of a heavy meal so the after-dinner pull isn't so strong. Plan journeys by different modes of transport if you know driving is a trigger. If you worry that among your friends there are smokers who might lure the quitter back, then tactfully ask them to keep out of the way for a while. If they have to come round, enforce a strict no-smoking rule. We're not advocating that you dump all your smoking friends for good; just keep them at arm's length for the first couple of weeks of quitting. After a while the quitter will be able to hang out with smokers again without feeling tempted, but don't rush it. During the first few days, even seeing another person smoke will trigger the urge, so try to minimize the chances of this happening.

Anticipate the old triggers and make sure they are kept out of the way by planning around them, and you'll make the quit road less bumpy. Help the quitter on a day-by-day basis by keeping some healthy snacks on hand, making sure there's a bottle of water by the telephone, or some mints by the bed so that, at those critical moments of temptation, there's an alternative option readily available. Buy them a lollipop, some sugar-free gum, mouthwash or a new toothbrush. Even better, take up a hobby together that keeps the hands occupied. Play cards instead of watching TV, do artwork, needlework, woodwork, a jigsaw, crossword puzzles – or decorate (or plan how you'll decorate) your new smoke-free living room.

- Do say: fancy going for a walk? Game of cards? Twister?
- Don't say: let's go down the pub for a few drinks.

RULE NO. 4:
Tolerate the Ups and Downs

Make no bones about it, the quitter may have some uncharacteristic mood swings and be more irritable, angry or emotional than usual. If this happens try to be as tolerant as you can. And don't criticize the quitter for the way they are behaving. Remind yourself that this is a phase, it's quite normal, it's worse for them than it is for you and it *will* pass. Even if their behaviour seems unreasonable, if you retaliate you're more likely to drive the person back to smoking. Whatever's going through your mind, never say, 'You were much easier to live with when you smoked.' Simply bite your tongue and know it will pass in a matter of days. If you see the person getting stressed or anxious, encourage them to use the many methods in this book to cope. Never, ever suggest they have 'just one' cigarette in the hope that it will relieve their mood. It won't and will only set them back several stages. This is a time for you to muster all the understanding, patience, compassion and tolerance you can. It may be a tough time for you but do remind yourself of the tremendous benefits that lie ahead for both of you and focus on your new healthier lifestyle. As the saying goes, no pain, no gain.

Don't get alarmed if the person trying to quit complains of all sorts of withdrawal symptoms, from dizziness to insomnia. These are merely the body's way of showing that it is becoming nicotine-free. They should be welcomed with open arms, not dread. Some quitters experience an increase in symptoms of anxiety and depression. Watch out for this in your partner and support them as much as you can. On the plus side, this programme is based around techniques that improve mood and reduce stress, so don't be surprised if the opposite effect occurs and the quitter is less anxious and less depressed. Sleep disturbances sometimes bother the quitter, too, as do concentration difficulties and general fatigue. The programme in this book, again, should minimize these withdrawal symptoms if the quitter sticks to it and also gets plenty of exercise. Most people say the first week is the worst and symptoms lessen after that. Just give them time to let the mood pass, without overreacting, even if you do secretly begin to wonder if your ex-smoker has been replaced by a raging monster. They will get back to their old self in time.

If you are the partner of a quitter and you smoke yourself, it goes without saying that this is a great opportunity for both of you to quit. And if you go through this programme together you will have great fun and revitalize your relationship, and enrich your lives at the same time. If your partner is going it alone, though, do make every effort not to smoke around them. Also keep your smokes hidden from view and out of reach. And finally never, ever offer them one again.

- Do say: it's tough now, but every day it'll get easier.
- Don't say: I preferred you when you smoked.

RULE NO. 5:
Familiarize Yourself with This Programme

The more you know about the Love Not Smoking: Do Something Different programme, the more you will be able to support your partner through it and help them to quit for good. Let us warn you: there are some pretty strange things that can happen when someone is on this programme, and we want you to be prepared for them. Most of all, we really want you to go along with the things your partner is doing. Don't throw a fit when they start to rearrange the furniture – it truly is part of the programme. Don't laugh or ridicule them when they are trying to lick their own elbow, cook kippers for breakfast or learn Mandarin; give them all the encouragement you can. And don't be surprised if they start behaving a little out of character. It shows they are sticking with the programme and taking its messages on board. And that means they'll be more likely to succeed. Just remember, these changes are necessary for them to embed new habits and shake off the old. There's no need to feel threatened by this; it's not about you.

The real and ultimate success of the programme depends on the person's ability to break all kinds of old habits (not just smoking), and that means they will be trying out some new behaviours now and again. Just sit back and watch with interest, and know that many people have gained life-enhancing benefits from these techniques. Better still, join in if you can. Don't feel threatened by these changes. You are not losing your partner, but getting them back, retuned, improved and reconditioned!

- Do say: what are you doing differently today – and can I help?
- Don't say: what on earth are you doing *that* for?

REMEMBER. If you are supporting someone through the quitting process, help them get the most from this programme with these pointers:

1. **Positive encouragement**

2. **Selfless motivation**

3. **Minimize temptation**

4. **Tolerate the ups and downs**

5. **Familiarize yourself with this programme.**

The Family Challenge

If you have kids, then why not let them take part in the Do Something Different tasks? They'll love the variety and the new experiences, and everyone in the family will benefit.

> Children's behaviours are naturally flexible. In fact, as adults we expend huge amounts of energy trying to tame them. But we can learn a lot from children.

Children can show us how to get unstuck from a rut. How to be more spontaneous. They can teach us not to worry about what others think, and how to see the fun in all we do. Look at how children jump at the chance to have a break from routine. They'll stay up late, skip a bath, wear silly hats, eat ice-cream for breakfast or sleep at the wrong end of the bed faster than you can say DSD. Contrast this with the way many adults have to be dragged kicking and screaming into just minor diversions from normality.

So let your kids join in, at least for the first couple of weeks of the programme. You could even ask them to make up more DSDs and create a challenge that the whole family can undertake. You could even share them with the Love Not Smoking support group to help other families (www.lovenotsmoking.com). Let them loose on the idea and encourage them to show you how you can shake up your routine. Kids love DSDs; they think they're 'awesome'. In our research we've found that DSD Family Challenges have the power to improve family functioning, enhance family cohesion and make parental stress a thing of the past.

Chapter 7

HOW I QUIT

Keith

Keith is 60 years old and had been a smoker since the tender age of 14. Last year he gave up smoking using the Do Something Different technique. A devoted granddad, it was love that finally drove Keith to make the decision to quit once and for all. As he went to light up a cigarette one day in the garden, his grandson, then aged nine, said to him, 'Don't smoke, Granddad. If you smoke, how are you going to play football with me when you're 70?' That, according to Keith, is when the true reality of what he was doing finally hit home. He suddenly felt foolish before this child that he loved, and said to himself, 'What am I doing?' Keith lives for his family and is devoted to them. 'We're very close, very caring and a real family unit. The grandchildren come and stay with us a lot, and my three granddaughters had started to nag me about smoking as well. That's when I gave up.' Keith's wife, Pauline, had always tolerated his smoking. A non-smoker herself, she knew no amount of nagging on her part would have made him quit, but always knew it was up to Keith to make the move when he wanted to.

When the time came, Keith started on the Love Not Smoking: Do Something Different programme and got a bit of a shock to find out he didn't have to stop smoking immediately. 'On the first day I was ready to trash the cigs, but found out all I had to do was not watch the telly!' Keith admitted he thought that was a tough task, but as it happened it coincided with a visit from the grandchildren. The youngest had a party coming up later that week and wanted to create a 'pin the nose on the clown' game. Keith got down on the floor with the kids, out came the felt-tip pens and paper, and what followed was an evening of hilarity as they set about seeing who could make the funniest clown.

I look back on that evening and still smile to myself. Usually I'd have watched the telly and just let the kids play around me. But with it turned off I didn't have much choice but to join in with them – and it was a smashing night. Their mum and dad had told them that I was giving up smoking, and all were overjoyed and very supportive of me. And they thought it was the best thing in the world to have Granddad's full attention. They still talk about it to this day. I didn't even feel the need to smoke. If I'm honest I probably ended up having a better time than them. It was such a trivial thing to do, I suppose, not watch telly, but it really started to open my eyes and made me think about what else I could do differently.

As he worked his way through the DSD programme, Keith started to become very aware of the habitual nature of many of the things he did every day.

I'd come downstairs in the morning, put the kettle on and have my first cig while it was boiling. Never gave it much thought, really, but I could have done it with my eyes closed. Kitchen, kettle, cigs and tea. That was me every day. Then my last smoke would be when I took the dog for a walk last thing at night. In between I was an 'advert smoker'. As soon as the adverts came on the telly, I'd pop outside and have a smoke. Like clockwork I suppose I was. Now I recognized that my weakness or habit was the adverts on telly, but if the telly is off life does not have adverts so I don't smoke so much! Remedy: turn the bloody telly off or just watch channels that do not have adverts!

Once I started doing DSD I'd still get up during the ad breaks, but I'd go somewhere else. I started going upstairs and would go and switch on the computer to take my mind off smoking. Just being in a different place made me want to smoke less, and keeping busy made a big difference. I couldn't have stopped with just a patch; I really needed to keep my hands and my mind busy.

Another habit that Keith managed to break was his regular daily routine of taking the newspaper outside, sitting down with a beer and having a cigarette. 'I'd get through about four cigs an hour during that time.' The need to do this disappeared once he found he had a skill on the computer for creating invitations and banners for special events. He now spends some of his time creating a portfolio of designs for family and friends, and his party stationery is in great demand.

Keith broke the association between the garden (where he'd always smoked) and his need for a cigarette by moving his cigarettes to the end of the garden during Week 2.

I always kept them on the windowsill by the back door, and would pick them up and light up just out the back. When I moved them to the shed at the end of the garden it made me think twice about whether I really wanted one or not. Sometimes I just didn't bother and went and did something else instead. A little thing as easy as that made all the difference.

By doing something different, Keith discovered a whole host of new interests. And having a way of keeping boredom at bay was, for him, the greatest asset when he gave up smoking. The variety of tasks gave him a new lease of life and he managed to adapt them to his own lifestyle.

I don't drive and always walk or use public transport, so the day the task was to walk instead of drive I made a point of walking a completely different route. I know not all the DSDs will suit everyone, but I found it really easy to mould them to fit around my own circumstances.

Although it's months now since Keith quit, he says he still keeps the programme handy, and every now and again will reread it or reach for his Habit-breaker Cards (available at www.lovenotsmoking.com).

The cards came in very handy. I got some funny looks once when I was queuing in a bank and standing on one leg, but they got me through the craving stage. Just finding something different to do is what it's all about; it made sense for me and even now I still

*keep them out for when I might need one. The old
associations don't just disappear overnight. At the
weekend we'd been into town and stopped at a pub
on the way home. We sat in the beer garden and I
could smell other people's smoke; there was beer and
tasty grub. In fact loads of the old associations were
there. I can't say I didn't think about smoking but I
knew there and then that I'd never have another one.
Ever. Anyway, food tastes much better now so that's
a good reason to enjoy eating out and not smoking.
Another one is that I actually sit through a whole meal
now! When I smoked I used to be thinking, 'Hurry up
and bring that soup so I can nip out for a smoke' and
then, 'I won't bother with pudding; I'll go and have a
smoke instead.' I was up and down from the table and
used to miss out on loads of the conversation – they
were probably talking about me! – but now I'm there
all the way through, and I think that's great for family
relationships.*

**New interests, more family time and better
relationships were just some of the advantages of
DSD for Keith.**

The programme also spurred Keith on to do something
different outside the home: he now is a volunteer for a
group that delivers food skills to the community.

*I've been given training, learned about nutrition and
food hygiene and how to teach. Food had begun to
taste so much better once I gave up smoking and
I found I loved to cook. Now I spend a few hours a
week passing on the skills and knowledge to young*

mums, helping them provide their kids with the best possible nutrition – even if they're on a budget. We cook together and then discuss nutrition and the best stuff they can afford for their kids. I know that by doing this we stand a chance of making a real difference to the future health of the children and it gives me a great sense of fulfilment and satisfaction.

A retired painter and decorator, Keith loves giving something back and doing different things. And we wouldn't be surprised if he were kicking a football around with his grandson when he's 70, and beyond.

Keith's smoking patterns were tied to all kinds of associations, contexts and triggers. Once he became aware of these and disrupted them by doing something different, smoking no longer had a strong grip on him and he was able to give up successfully after more than 40 years of a so-called addiction.

Chapter 8

HOW TO FOLLOW THE PROGRAMME

Love Not Smoking: Do Something Different is a complete programme with six stages. But don't let that put you off, because it's really just as simple as doing one thing each day. Something that's a bit different to what you'd normally do. We'll tell you each day what that is, and you do it. It's really as straightforward and easy to follow as that.

> Each stage lasts a week or so, and we walk you through every single step of the way, day by day. It will become your road map on the way to a smoke-free life, with every stage carefully worked out for you.

One reason people tell us they like this programme is the daily tasks are set out for them. This is important because we know that the brain's main default setting makes it hard for us to think and act differently. So this programme gives you all the changes needed to readjust the default setting, one day at a time. And they're quite uncomplicated changes, too. That's not to say you can't mould the tasks to suit your own lifestyle and personal circumstances. Just remember to keep the Do Something Different spirit alive when you do so, and don't snuggle back into your comfort zone.

As you work through the programme, you'll probably start to feel how it is subtly and gradually reprogramming your life and your mind. OK, there will be times when you stop and wonder why on earth we're asking you to do the things you're doing, like when you're rearranging the furniture, listing insects, spotting caravans or making an apple last ten minutes, but trust us. There is a solid foundation to these techniques and you will start to feel better and enjoy injecting some variety into your life. The programme nudges you toward the all-round healthier lifestyle of a non-smoker because, as the scientist Arthur Winter has pointed out, 'For your brain to thrive, it needs exercise, nourishment and protection from toxins.' Best of all, when you do finally stop smoking on the third week, once and for all, you won't feel bereft (as you secretly dreaded you might). Your life will already have undergone several subtle shifts and there simply won't be a place in it for smoking.

As you might have guessed, we had a sound rationale for designing a programme that lasts for six weeks. It gives you time to commit to a quit date two weeks in advance, and four weeks' support through the first month of non-smoking.

> **Whatever you do, don't wait for the 'right time' to quit. There is no such thing. The right time to start preparing to quit is now, and reasons for not doing so are mere excuses.**

Research has shown that setting a date and making it public increases the likelihood of your succeeding, and that two weeks is the right amount of time to prepare.

Also, when Anna Mertziani studied research statistics on successful quits, she concluded that 'Intensive methods, extended for longer periods are more effective than briefer forms of behavioural interventions.' Added to that, it has been shown that after four weeks the body is free of nicotine and withdrawal symptoms (for those who've had them) have completely subsided. So that's why we're giving you a six-week programme, with two weeks' intensive preparation and four weeks of support post-quit. Since this is a daily programme, we suggest you keep this book with you throughout the whole six-week period, or have it in a handy place so you know exactly where to find it when you need it. It is going to be your friend, guide, bible and partner over the next few weeks. If you are also using the Love Not Smoking app, make sure you start it at the same time. And don't forget to join our support group on www.lovenotsmoking.com.

First, let's take a look at a brief sum-up of the whole programme.

Week 1: Preparation

This gets you ready for change and gives you time to prepare and plan for quitting smoking. You'll try some simple Do Something Different activities to show you that you can give your usual routines a bit of a shake-up. We're going to proceed in small incremental steps so that when we've loosened up the hold that your habits have on you, smoking will be much easier to give up.

Week 2: Know Your Smoking Triggers

This stage really does open your eyes to all the trivial, everyday habits that have crept under your mental radar and that your brain has connected with smoking. You'll start to notice the subtle associations between the things you do – the places you go to, the people you hang out with, what and how you eat and even the words you use – and the mindless automatic-ness of smoking. You'll work on breaking up those subconscious connections. So just because you're in a certain place or doing a particular thing, you don't have to smoke. This will start to disrupt the links and help you to unlearn past associations that have been sneaking up on you and triggering your smoking. With some gentle mind-training and better understanding of your smoking cues, you'll already be on the way to quit.

Week 3: Time to Quit

This is No-Smoking Week 1, and you'll stop smoking on the first day of this week. Most quitters find it's easier to stop all in one go rather than to cut down gradually, so no-more-cigs time has definitely arrived. You'll have reached your target date for quitting and now, instead of smoking, you'll be *doing something different*. This continues the process of readjustment, reconditioning the brain not to expect a shot of nicotine every time it bumps into the usual triggers. Physical withdrawal affects different people in different ways, and is known to peak at around Day 2 or 3 as all nicotine is removed from the body. The steps in this phase of the programme help you beat the cravings and counter the pull of past habits.

Week 4: Adding New Behaviours

This is No-Smoking Week 2. You'll begin to see how DSD helps you stay busy and focused as your brain becomes sensitized to new cues. You'll be starting to learn how to increase your behavioural flexibility, to make conscious choices and not live your life on autopilot. And the process of extinguishing those old triggers and relearning will continue to make sure you don't slip back into your old ways.

Week 5: Changing Habits

This is No-Smoking Week 3. Research shows that within two or three weeks of quitting, the brain readjusts to living without nicotine. So by this stage you'll really be feeling you've broken free of the grip of smoking and, boy, how much better life is without it. If you can contain your exuberance at this stage, the programme now helps you consolidate the new learning that your subconscious mind has undergone, by tackling your habits to do with 'Relationships' and 'Activity'. You'll develop better habits in your everyday life and continue to act more consciously, to be more in control.

At this point many people are so delighted with the results, and find they love being a non-smoker so much, that they can exit the full programme. In which case there's a simple seven-day Do Something Different-a-Day programme to finish up with, so that you don't become a creature of habit (any habit) again and continue to blaze a smokeless trail. That starts on page 249. Or you can continue with the programme to Week 6.

Week 6 (Optional): Transformation

This part of the programme is for those who want to learn more about how behaviour optimization can develop them as a person. This has lots of benefits in many aspects of your life, your inner world and your outer relationships. It puts you in charge of your personality instead of it controlling you. But it does require dedication and insight, and isn't for the faint-hearted. It is, however, for people who don't just want to give up smoking but have realized the power of Do Something Different in helping them shape the course of their life, and want to carry on reaping the benefits.

Relapse-Prevention Week

After that there's a **stay smoke-free week** (in Chapter 9), just to keep you on course and support you farther along the road on which you've started. It's a practical relapse-prevention week that you can implement at any time you wish.

Finally, this book isn't just about smoking. It's also a personal development programme and has an emphasis on love (hence the title). So in Chapter 11 you'll find some ways to *nurture your relationship* and make sure that love, not smoking, is what you put your energies into as life moves ahead.

Before You Say, 'This isn't for me'

If when you are looking through this programme (and let's face it, who ever starts a book at the beginning and reads right through to the end? We all have a peek first to see what we're letting ourselves in for) you think *This isn't for me*, can we ask that you suspend that judgement just for a little longer? Instead, ask yourself, how could I adapt and apply these techniques so they fit my life right now? You don't have to do every task set, or in the way they are described here. You can modify them so they are more suited to your lifestyle and your need for control. You don't even have to do them in the order they're listed in this book. Feel free to dip in and out and around the book as much as you like. Make it your own and see how you can get the best out of each exercise. Use the app (www.lovenotsmoking.com) for instant, portable nuggets of advice. Just know that if you can adapt and apply the universal principles of Do Something Different in your quest to quit smoking, we know you'll never look back. Ask yourself, 'What have I got to lose by giving it a try?' You have only your smoking to lose, and in return your health, long life, more money and the appreciation and peace of mind of your loved ones to gain.

As Mark Twain famously said, 'Twenty years from now you will be more disappointed by the things that you didn't do than by the ones you did do. So throw off the bowlines. Sail away from the safe harbour. Catch the trade winds in your sails. Explore. Dream. Discover.'

Part II

THE SIX-WEEK LOVE NOT SMOKING: DO SOMETHING DIFFERENT PROGRAMME

OK, this is where you start the programme, and the very first thing you are going to do is to work out your Target Quit Date. That will be the first day on which you won't smoke a single cigarette. It'll be a really significant and important day for you, the start of freedom and a healthier future, so we want you to record it below.

The date should be two weeks after you begin the programme. So, if you're ready to start the programme tomorrow, your Target Quit Date will be two weeks from tomorrow.

Don't be tempted to dive in straight away and go cold turkey. You'll find it easier to give up if you have a couple of weeks to plan and prepare. And during that time we'll start to unravel your habit web so that quitting is easier. Don't leave it any longer than two weeks, though – you can't put it off forever!

MY TARGET QUIT DATE

February 1st, 2022

If you are using the Love Not Smoking app, you should now enter the same target quit date.

If you don't have the app, it's not too late to download it. Visit www.lovenotsmoking.com for details.

Broadcast the Date

Can we also suggest you write that date on a few pieces of paper and stick them in strategic places? Record it in your diary, on your phone or mark it on the calendar.

Next you are going to decide whom you will tell about your plan to quit smoking. The more you broadcast it, the more likely it is to happen. So, short of stopping people on the street, shouting from the rooftops or having it tattooed on your forehead, we encourage you to tell as many people as possible. Let all your friends and family know, as well as everyone with whom you work. Create a support network of people who will be behind you every step of the way. Tell them what you're doing and why, and let them know your Target Quit Date. Muster their moral support as well as any help they are able to offer. Another way to announce you're quitting is to send friends and family an e-card. You can find these on the internet, for example at www.nosmokingday.org. uk. Or you could post your target quit date on our support group (visit www.lovenotsmoking.com), to tell your friends, family, fellow quitters, and us.

Most importantly, IGNORE anyone who:

- Says you won't be able to do it
- Tells you they've tried and failed
- Doubts you have the strength to see it through

There will always be cynics out there who might question whether you've got it in you to quit this time. They may even secretly want you to fail, maybe because they're a smoker themselves and don't want to lose a fellow smoker. Perhaps they wrongly believe that you won't be the same person if you stop smoking; that you'll change in some way and they're worried about what that may mean for them. Others around you may even misguidedly think that smoking helps you to cope with the pressures of life. Whatever their reasons, they are *not your* reasons and you have to tune out what those naysayers say. *Turn a deaf ear* if they try to remind you of your previous failed attempts – that's all behind you now – or if they try to talk you out of quitting. Instead:

- Stay around people who want to *support and encourage you*, the believers. Those are the people who really matter because they want what's best for you.
- Befriend an ex-smoker. If you know someone who's quit successfully, enlist their help along the way or simply call on them when you need encouragement.
- Know someone else who wants to quit? Buddy up and do it together. Ideal for those of a competitive nature. Or just to have fun swapping experiences, doing the daily tasks or the new activities together. Who knows? You will probably deepen your friendship as a result.

Professor Richard Wiseman has studied the psychology of motivation, and in his book *59 Seconds* he reports on the techniques that have helped people achieve a major life change:

> *Successful participants were more likely than others to tell their friends, family and colleagues about their goals. It seems that although keeping your aims to yourself helps ease the fear of failure, it also makes it too easy to avoid changing your life and drift back into old habits and routines.*

> Forget all your previous unsuccessful quit attempts,
> if you have had them. The fact that you have tried to
> quit before has absolutely no bearing on your ability
> to quit with the Love Not Smoking: Do Something
> Different programme.

Jot down the name(s) of your supporters here (these
are the people you are going to tell about your Target
Quit Date):

- Everyone!
- Esp. Grandpa, Baba, Brendlyn,
Dad, Mom, Madi, Auntie -
Justin Stephanie -

Now begin.

PREPARATION

The next step is to create a No-Smoking Zone in your personal environment, home or surroundings. This will target one of your smoking associations and start to disrupt the environmental triggers that have been supporting your smoking.

Creating a No-Smoking Zone involves two steps.

Step 1: Pick a Place to Be Your No-Smoking Zone

- Pick a place where you would normally smoke regularly – this could be a room in your house where you usually smoke, your car or somewhere at work.
- Make it your No-Smoking Zone. It is now a place where you will not smoke a single cigarette, or even enter with cigarettes on you.
- You can carry on smoking elsewhere for the time being, just not in this place.

Step 2: Convert the Place into a Smoke-Free Zone

Now convert the place that you have chosen into a smoke-free environment. You might like to:

- Refresh and clean and tidy the room/space and let in some fresh air
- Put some fresh flowers in, use a plug-in air freshener (or buy one for the car)

- Remove all ashtrays or fill them with scented pot-pourri (from dried flowers or fragrant herbs)
- Put coins or sweets in your car ashtray
- Install some house plants to filter the air
- Burn some incense or aromatherapy oils
- Put in an ionizer to boost levels of negative ions in the air
- Make sure that whenever you go into that room/place you don't even have your cigarettes on you
- Don't let anybody else smoke in that room

Now Decide

Which place are you going to turn into a No-Smoking Zone this week?

Write it here .....my....patio...(weed......
                                        allowed)

What to Do Next

Now think about what you'll do to make sure your chosen place remains a non-smoking zone. For this to be really effective, the more actions you take, the better.

Next, tick the actions that you are going to take in order to convert one place into a No-Smoking Zone:

Actions

1.	Clean the room/place	☐
2.	Refresh it/open windows and let in the fresh air	☐
3.	Remove all ashtrays	☐
4.	Be in that room/place without any cigarettes on you	☐

5. Fill any ashtrays with coins/sweets/
   flowers, etc. ☐
6. Do not allow anyone else to smoke there ☐
7. Put up a No Smoking sign ☐
8. Introduce flowers, plants, incense and/or
   air freshener ☐
9. Or do something different (write it here):

....

Research has shown that the more reminders of smoking you have around you, the greater the chance that you'll relapse. So the No-Smoking Zone is critical and you should think about gradually rolling this out and making everywhere around you a No-Smoking Zone once you quit. You will find it much easier to become a quitter if you aim to get rid of all nicotine products, ashtrays, lighters, matches and start completely afresh. We promise you, it'll feel like a breath of fresh air.

Week 1

SMALL CHANGES

Now you've created your No-Smoking Zone, you're going to start disrupting some of your normal everyday habits and ringing the changes. Just to remind you, the idea of this is to begin to break up the habit web that has been supporting your smoking. Remember, once the web falls apart, your smoking drops away, too. So each step of this programme is important if that's to happen.

That's why the Love Not Smoking: Do Something Different programme targets two different aspects of your life:

1. Your general everyday life – the little routines and ways you go about doing things that seem to have nothing to do with smoking.
2. Your smoking behaviour specifically – the when, where and why of smoking.

This two-pronged attack is crucial because your smoking is tangled up with lots of other aspects of your life. You will have learned to associate many of the things that you do and that happen to you, with smoking. That's why the Love Not Smoking: Do Something Different programme aims to slowly undermine and then break those links, so you find it easier not to smoke.

So this first week starts to chip away at those habits. Don't look ahead too much, just take one day at a time. The daily tasks involve removing one or two incidental things that have become habits, trying new things and considering simple alternatives. If you can go into it with an open mind, ready to have some fun and daring to be different, you'll get a lot out of it.

What You Have to Do

- There is a page for each day that you are on the Love Not Smoking: Do Something Different programme. This will tell you what to do that day.
- Have a go at the tasks you are set each day. Try not to miss a day.
- If you do have to miss a day, carry on where you left off. If you are also using the Love Not Smoking app, make sure it is synchronized with the correct day of your programme.

Remember, by sticking to the set tasks and regularly following the programme, you'll have a much higher chance of success. But if you can't stick to them in the way they are in the book, feel free to adapt them to suit you. Share your experiences and any personal techniques and tips with your fellow quitters in our exclusive support group at www.lovenotsmoking.com.

In Week 1 you have one task each day.

We do appreciate it may seem strange to you that the Love Not Smoking: Do Something Different programme tackles all sorts of basic everyday habits. Trivial things like the seat you sit in, what you choose off a menu or the way you travel to work. You might wonder what on earth some of these activities have got to do with smoking. That's a reasonable thought to have. But we hope you'll come to see that turning some of these everyday routines and automatic behaviours – many of the things we do without thinking – upside down is the key to bringing about the bigger changes in your life. Our research shows that habits are obstacles to people getting what they want because willpower is too weak to overcome them. Your subconscious mind has built up a whole host of different associations that have led it to expect nicotine at particular times, or in specific contexts or locations. Doing something different breaks the chains of habits and extinguishes the cues that have conditioned you to smoke. Nicotine isn't the only enemy within, there's inertia, too.

Don't Forget Your Toothbrush!

If you want to test out the strength of your own automatic behaviour, try this.

Move your toothbrush from its usual place in the bathroom to a different place. If it's by the sink, move it to the windowsill. If it's on a shelf, put it into a cupboard. Then, every time you clean your teeth, notice where you go to first to get your toothbrush. We'll wager you keep going back to the old place.

It's not that you don't know where your toothbrush is now. It's because your brain has learned an automatic pattern and has encoded it in a well-worn pathway. One you don't have to think about. When you send a 'toothbrush-search' instruction to your brain, it just automatically activates the old pathway. It can take several days to learn the new route.

Without these pathways we'd have to think consciously about every tiny thing we do. That would overload the brain hugely, so we 'automatize' a lot of routine stuff. So every time you get dressed you don't have to think about whether your shoes go on after your socks or your socks go on after your shoes. You do it all without thinking, without effort, and that's good. It means you can carry on a conversation at the same time as dressing. You can be planning what you're going to say at a meeting while putting on your shoes and socks. Cognitive capacity is freed up by automatic-ness; that's what makes us the flexible, multitasking, thinking human beings that we are. But sometimes, when we want to change behaviour, we need to force some of those automatic habits into conscious awareness. Once we're aware of them we can try to redirect ourselves down a different pathway. Here, instead of automatically smoking, you'll be learning how to divert yourself down a different, smoke-free pathway. And with time that new pathway will become the default, making the old one redundant. That's what doing something different helps you to do.

Day 1   Date: ...Jan 18th...
YOUR TASK FOR TODAY

No watching TV all day (if you are not a TV watcher, cut out the radio)

Your first go at habit-busting: no TV. This may be a difficult start for some of you, but give it a try and think about what you can do instead of watching TV. Notice how much extra time you seem to have and how much you get done in that time.

We're asking you to turn it off just for today. Research shows that people who watch television may find it relaxing and easy to do but, because they are passive, it does not provide any stimulation of the kind that constitutes pleasure. Real pleasure comes from active engagement with life, and television (like alcohol) tends to put a distance between us and the real world – whatever 'reality' television would have you believe. It has even been shown that people get more out of work than watching television.

Over time, watching TV can suck your life away without you even noticing. You mentally switch off every time you switch on. You fail to notice time passing and slip into automatic mode. We (Ben and Karen) try very hard to be what we teach. So we turned our TV off seven years ago and haven't watched one since. You might think that's a bit extreme, but we feel we've been given our lives back. We spend our evenings preparing and enjoying meals (always candlelit), having hearty discussions, reading, exercising, painting, listening to music, devising new projects, making bread, looking at art, doing crossword puzzles, writing, playing Scrabble, growing herbs, going to the cinema or live events, or being with friends. We marvel that people have time to watch television, or that they would even *want* to.

But we're not asking you to give up TV for good! Just for one day. See what can happen if you break a simple habit.

Plan one or two things that you might do instead:

- Call an old friend.
- Prepare tomorrow's breakfast or packed lunch.
- Read a book.
- Do a crossword or other puzzle.
- Go out for a walk or run.
- Clean or tidy a drawer or cupboard.
- Listen to music.

We are not saying here that watching TV is the reason why you smoke. We are saying that if you stay trapped in habitual ways of doing things then you'll find it harder to quit smoking. Watching TV is just an example of one of these habits; see if you can break it for one day. Then see if you can Do Something Different.

Nicole, 28: I don't usually spend lots of time watching TV, but knew I had to make this task my own. So I decided to apply it to a habit that takes up most of my free time, preventing me from doing important things, and where I used to light up all the time ... on the computer. I used to be addicted to Facebook. It was refreshing and a real eye-opener to see what I could get sorted in the time I would usually spend on the PC – and it even meant I cut down on the amount I smoked.

Day 2   Date: Jan 19th
YOUR TASK FOR TODAY

Go for a 15-minute walk at the beginning or end of your day

This simple task is one that most people find makes a big difference. All you have to do is go for a short walk, either at the beginning or the end of your day. Really try to make time to do this and, ideally, fit it in before you get settled into your normal routine. So maybe do it straight away when you get in from work or – if you're a morning person – as soon as you're up and dressed. You might be surprised at the difference it makes to how you're feeling. Notice how it clears your head, particularly after a busy or stressful day, and how it refreshes you.

This could be just the beginning of a healthier daily habit. It's certainly a good idea to get your exercise rate up as much as you can before you give up smoking. Keeping active will boost your chances enormously of staying off cigarettes. Exercise will focus the mind, raise your motivation and lift your mood. It has also been shown to reduce the cravings felt by quitters. Physical activity also results in a stronger flow of blood, glucose and oxygen to the brain, and helps stimulate the growth of new neurons. So keep moving!

If you're giving up because you're pregnant, the Love Not Smoking: Do Something Different programme is a safe, positive alternative to drugs or nicotine replacement therapy. Scientists still have some concerns that nicotine replacement may harm the foetus, because pregnant women metabolize nicotine a lot faster than others. Researchers from St George's Hospital in London found that pregnant women who exercised regularly were as successful at quitting as non-pregnant women using nicotine replacement therapy. So add regular exercise to the Love Not Smoking programme and you'll find packing it in far easier as you also protect your unborn baby, maintain a healthy weight and give your self-image a boost.

Day 3   Date: ....Jan 20.....
YOUR TASK FOR TODAY

Have breakfast (if you normally have breakfast, try eating something new)

Some people (especially smokers) are happy with just a mug of coffee and a couple of cigarettes first thing in the morning. Nicotine releases stored fats and sugars into the bloodstream and alleviates blood-sugar swings. Today we want you to relearn a new and healthier way of starting the day, with a good breakfast. This will refuel the body when you wake, kick-start your metabolism and begin a much healthier morning routine. It's also an excellent habit to start cultivating now, because when you stop smoking you must make sure you don't skip meals. Try to start a new habit of having small, healthy but regular meals.

Today, why not prepare something that you have always wanted to have for breakfast but haven't had time for before? A bowl of fresh fruit, a smoothie, some porridge, muesli, oatcakes or scrambled eggs. This may mean shopping for some fresh ingredients, or getting up earlier, but put some real effort into breakfast today.

To make it extra special, how about breakfast in bed on a tray, breakfast in the garden, a candlelit breakfast or going out to breakfast with a friend? Preferably one who doesn't smoke and has healthy food tastes – this isn't the time to make for the nearest greasy spoon!

Lisa, 34: My breakfast usually consisted of a cup of coffee and a smoke. I would then have the shakes by 12 and gorge on anything I could find. Not helpful if, like me, you struggle with your weight, too. I had none of these symptoms on Day 3 of the programme and realized that a proper breakfast would be more useful to me than what I usually had.

Day 4   Date: ...Jan 21st

YOUR TASK FOR TODAY

Write something for 15 minutes

Do you rarely express your thoughts in writing? When was the last time you put pen to paper and allowed the words to flow onto a page? Today you're going to do just that. Try to write for 15 minutes about something you would not normally write down. Don't contemplate at length what it should be or worry too much about the content, just let your thoughts flow naturally and uncensored. You could start a story, a memoir, a poem or your own autobiography. You don't have to judge it or show it to anyone; just express yourself. Even writing down your worries can help to put life in perspective, and listing all the things in life for which you are grateful can lift your mood.

Some people believe that smoking is a necessary way of achieving relaxation or coping with the stresses and worries in life. That's because they are tricked into feeling a sense of relief when they light up a cigarette, but it's a relief from the craving of nicotine that they feel, and this gets misinterpreted as a reduction in stress levels. Millions of non-smokers handle stress successfully without using cigarettes. Writing down your worries can be a simple way of putting them in perspective. Many people say they feel a sense of relief from doing this, without the need for a smoke.

Linda, 41: This was my opportunity to say goodbye to my trusted friend, which I had used in so many ways to cope. I wrote a poem to express my feelings and focused on the new start I was making to improve my health and emotional wellbeing.

Day 5   Date: Jan 22nd
YOUR TASK FOR TODAY

Eat something you have not had before

Today's the day to branch out, tickle your taste buds and try something completely new and out of the ordinary. It might be an unusual fruit or vegetable, or a dish from another culture. When we're out and about in different areas we love to pop into shops that serve an ethnic minority community, perhaps a Lebanese, Polish or Bangladeshi grocer's. The sheer range of new sights and smells stimulates the senses and excites the brain's synapses. Also, people are so helpful if you ask them what things are and how you should cook with them. Try to put any prejudices or preconceived ideas aside and open your mind to a fresh and different experience. You might like it. This is also your chance to swap your usual snack of crackers or cookies for something healthier, like raw vegetable sticks or dried fruit. You could stock up on some to have when you're no longer smoking.

Greek researchers studied the tongues of 62 soldiers (now, *there's* an unusual way to spend your time). They found that the tongues of the smokers had been physically changed by smoking. The smokers' tongues had fewer taste buds and were different in form, too, being flatter, which is associated with a reduced blood supply and less sensitivity, basically dulling the sensation of taste. Whether this was a good or bad thing might depend on your view of Greek food, but it might remind you that a whole host of new taste sensations await you when your taste buds are no longer disabled by nicotine.

Margie, 75: At my age I thought it was impossible to teach this old dog new tricks. I bought some kiwi fruit from my local shop. I sliced the top off, spooned out the juicy inside and enjoyed the taste tremendously. I now have a couple every day, which is incredible if you take into account that I don't usually eat any fruit at all.

Day 6   Date: Jan 23rd
YOUR TASK FOR TODAY

Rediscover your legs!

In modern society we over-depend on our cars to the point where we may sometimes look down at those appendages dangling from our lower body and wonder what they were for. Today is the day to rediscover your legs, to rely less on machines and exert some pedal power. Resist the temptation to use your car and consider using public transport instead. That way you will walk part of your journey, to the bus stop or station. If you really must drive, park farther away than you need to and then walk. It always amuses us how we try to park as near as possible when we go to the gym – ironic since the whole point of going there is to get some exercise. Yet we always try to make a point of walking up and down escalators. You could get off the bus early and walk part of your journey. And never, ever use an elevator. Take the stairs instead. If the floor is too high, then get out halfway and walk. Using an elevator to come down is inexcusable if you're able-bodied.

At work, get a bit more exercise by going to the most distant restroom instead of the one closest to your office/workspace. Just remember to allow yourself some extra time, or that cross-legged dash through accounts might raise a few eyebrows! When you're at home, go up and down the stairs at least once every hour. If you're getting older and sometimes forget what you went up there for, consider it a bonus. Those repeated trips mean you get more of a workout than most!

Research from the University of Bath has found that physical exercise reduces smokers' cravings for nicotine. The more ways you can find to raise your activity levels, the easier you'll find it to crush the smoking habit for good. If it's a struggle to find the energy at first, start slowly and don't be put off. Just remind yourself that giving up smoking increases your energy levels so things really can only get better.

> *Hannah, 33:* I realize I used to smoke to deal with low moods and unhappy feelings, thinking the cigs were going to help solve my problems. By adding activity to my daily routine, I noticed that this feel-good feeling of improving my life and using activity as a way to deal with stress and low mood was a much better way than having to rely on smoking.

Day 7   Date: Jan 24th
YOUR TASK FOR TODAY

Skip your favourite beverage

Having a cup of tea or coffee a dozen times a day can be as habitual for some people as breathing. We've come across folks who tell us they find themselves putting on the kettle without even thinking about whether or not they really want a drink. You may know people like that, or be one yourself, or perhaps you're someone who always has to have a can of cola on the go? How did we let ourselves become so umbilically attached to a mere beverage?

So, just for today, you are going to cut out your favourite regularly consumed drink. If you drink tea or coffee, give it a miss today. You don't need to go thirsty, because there are lots of alternatives to try and regular fluid intake is a good habit to adopt. But just for a change, why not avoid the coffee machine at work and take in some fruit juice? Or head for the water cooler instead? There's nothing better than water to flush the nicotine out of your system. Try herbal or green teas. Fruit juices will help you to remove nicotine, too, and they stabilize blood sugar. Cranberry juice is said to be particularly good. So enjoy taking a small habit and making a difference – and see if you can't kick-start a new habit, too, in the process.

Notice if your body reacts to not having something it's used to – caffeine withdrawal is just a demonstration of another type of habit (like nicotine withdrawal for the smoker). But it is also another example of a conditioned habit, so see if you gain some insight into another of your automatic behaviour patterns when you disrupt this one.

Certain drinks have been shown to affect how cigarettes taste to the smoker. A cold glass of milk makes them taste worse, according to research from the Duke University Medical Center. So having a glass of cold milk instead of coffee could be your secret weapon to breaking the habit, and this may work for other dairy products, too – consider putting more cheese and yoghurt in the fridge.

Now would be a good time to think about your intake of alcohol, too. Unfortunately, behind many smoking relapses lies an alcoholic drink. Or ten. All manner of virtuous intentions and inhibitions get blown to the wind when we've downed a few glasses of our favourite tipple. And nicotine and alcohol, when used in combination, each add to the kick of the other, according to research from the University of California San Francisco. The combined intake of a drink and a cigarette creates a link between them such that just having one can spark off a mammoth craving for the other. So you could be making it tougher for yourself if you drink while trying to stop smoking. Nine out of ten smokers in our survey said that an alcoholic drink triggered their desire for a cigarette. Avoid the drink and the trigger is weakened. If that sounds a bit drastic and you're wondering if there's going to be any fun left at all in your life, remember it's only for a short while. And if you Do Something Different you really can find plenty of other ways to get your kicks.

So, without sounding too much like your moralizing, teetotaling granny, can we suggest that from now on you practise spacing your alcoholic drinks farther apart, having booze-free days and finding non-alcoholic substitutes? Do this now and, we promise you, you'll have a strong back-up plan to see you through the quit period and minimize your chances of an alcohol-induced relapse.

Week 2

KNOW YOUR SMOKING TRIGGERS

I quit smoking, but I still get the urge when I stand outside an office building in the freezing cold.

The line above was the caption to a cartoon we spotted recently. It's funny, but it also shows that smoking triggers run deep.

So far you've already started to disrupt some habits, try new things and consider simple alternatives. That's good. At this stage, people often tell us they found the first week fairly easy and even had some pleasant surprises. 'I turned off the TV and phoned an old friend; we're getting together for dinner next week.' 'I'm a bit of a couch potato but my 15-minute walk turned into half an hour and I've kept it up ever since!' 'I wrote a poem about why I'm giving up, showed it to my kids and it was really moving.'

Remember, the aim of the programme is to give your normal habits a shake-up, to get rid of those smoking triggers and to interrupt your autopilot. This week will help you to stay alert to those sneaky old habits.

What You Have to Do Next

- For Week 2, each page again has a regular Do
  Something Different task for you to do that day.
- In addition, for each day there is a task specifically
  designed to disrupt your smoking habits. That's
  your Smoking-Disruptor Task.
- Try not to miss a day. But, if you do, just carry on
  where you left off.

Now it's time to think of all the situations that trigger you to light up a cigarette. Research shows that
smokers don't actually enjoy every single cigarette they
smoke. In fact, very few are really pleasurable, and lots
aren't even noticed. Many of the cigarettes you smoke
are smoked due to pure habit, not enjoyment.

What sort of smoking habits are there? You may recognize some of these:

- Lighting up a cigarette automatically, without even
  thinking about whether you wanted one or not
- Taking a cigarette that someone offers, even if
  you've only just finished one
- Particular places that are associated with smoking:
  the pub garden, perhaps, the bus stop or station
  platform
- Situations that automatically seem to trigger
  smoking: seeing someone else light up a cigarette,
  putting your hand in your pocket and feeling your
  cigarette packet, finishing a meal or answering the
  telephone

Smoke Rings

The 'smoke rings' we're talking about here are made up of the chains of habits in a smoker's life. A typical one might consist of waking up, having a cup of coffee, sitting down at the kitchen table, opening the newspaper and then lighting up a cigarette. Or another might be reaching for the cigs as soon as you finish a task and shut your computer. Perhaps you get in the car, start the engine, put the radio on and then light up. There's a rigid, pre-programmed sequence engrained in your behaviour and your brain has learned to dance to that tune. That means that when you perform the first habits in the chain, smoking is the inevitable last link. This stage of the programme is going to awaken you to the everyday events, situations and routines that so far have dictated when and how you smoke.

Up until now you may have felt that the urge to smoke came from within. It might have felt to you like a physiological or emotional state that was compelling you to have a cigarette. A bit like an itch that you simply have to scratch. Yet there is a lot of evidence from the scientific literature that the urge to smoke is cued *externally* rather than *internally*. Being surrounded by other smokers and by cigarettes, lighters and ashtrays will make it harder to fight the urge to smoke. That's one reason why we'll encourage you to remove all smoking paraphernalia once you stop. But the external cues aren't just smoking-related, and are present in a range of contexts. That's why we want you to understand and explore some of these this week.

The following questions will help you spot your most vulnerable smoking habits – those times and places when you smoke almost automatically, without thinking about it. Then, during the course of this week, you'll be on red alert as you watch out for your most powerful smoking triggers. This will be the first step to taking control of them, with the goal being to become conscious of your behaviour, unlearn your smoking responses and quit. You will understand how your behaviours guide your impulses because once you have that insight and level of control you will be able to choose how to act instead of being at the command of automatic forces.

Think of the smoke ring like a stack of dominoes stood on end. When you hit the first one, a whole chain of events is set in action, so that each one in turn falls. Now imagine turning one of the dominoes on its side. That stops the chain reaction and the rest remain standing. Your smoking habit is at the end of that line, and we are going to interrupt the sequence.

Have a look at the list that follows and check off any smoking habits that apply to you.

	Smoking Habit	Check
1	Smoking a cigarette just after I finish something	✓
2	Smoking a cigarette before I start something	✓
3	Smoking with my coffee	✓
4	Smoking while having an alcohol drink	✓
5	Smoking after I have finished a meal	✓
6	Smoking while listening to music or to a special song	
7	Smoking while driving	✓
8	Smoking while watching TV, or a movie	
9	Smoking while talking on the phone	✓
10	Smoking while working or studying	
11	Smoking while waiting	✓
12	Smoking while surfing the internet	
13	Smoking due to some emotional state (feeling stressed, sad, happy, awkward, etc.)	✓
14	Smoking while chatting with friends, socializing	✓
15	Smoking because I am bored	✓

You'll be very aware of how smoking goes hand in hand with other things you are doing or particular contexts such as having a coffee, after a meal, while chatting or socializing and so on. But different smokers have different sets of smoking habits and triggers, things that set the chain in progress. Whatever your strongest smoking habits might be, this week's goal is to disrupt this automatic response.

What You Have to Do Next

Each day you will learn to use a disrupting technique whenever you are about to light up a cigarette.

The idea of these disruptors is to draw your attention to the smoking context and help you spot the trigger. We are not asking you to stop smoking yet, but if these disruptors have that effect, go with it!

Day 8   Date: Jan 25th
YOUR TASK FOR TODAY

Practise a new relaxation technique

Many smokers believe smoking keeps them calm and holds stress at bay. The reason they feel this is that smoking does relieve the stress that builds up from nicotine addiction. But it doesn't relieve the stress of life; that's simply an illusion. It merely relieves the stress of craving a smoke. After all, non-smokers are not walking around in a constant state of stress, so nicotine is definitely not the answer. You need to find alternative responses to the feelings that make you believe you are stressed. Smoking is passive mood management, but learning how to relax yourself is an active method, giving you the means of control. If you have ever tried yoga or meditation, now is a good time to take it up again. Brush up on those old techniques, throw down a mat, light some incense and make it a regular practice again.

Alternatively, get into the habit of using this simple relaxation technique:

*   **Breathe in** slowly to the count of four.
*   **Breathe out** slowly to the count of four.

This is your basic relaxation breath. Just breathe as slowly and **comfortably** as you can. Counting gives you some idea of the right pace of your relaxed breathing. After you have the timing right, say **R-E-L-A-X** slowly to yourself each time you breathe out. Do this for about five minutes.

If you keep this up you will develop an association between the feeling of relaxation that you produce by using the above technique and the self-instruction RELAX. This is like the feeling that comes over you when you sit in front of an open fire. You associate the fire with pleasant relaxation. Relaxation also lowers the levels of cortisol in the body, which is associated with anxiety and stress. So you can use the above technique in a similar way to control feelings of anxiety or cravings. You will begin to associate the feelings of relaxation with the word RELAX, and the sensations of that slow, calm outward breath.

Patrick Reynolds, of Foundation for a Smokefree America, reckons that deep breathing is perhaps the single most important and powerful technique for successfully quitting cigarette smoking. So it's a habit worth cultivating.

YOUR SMOKING-DISRUPTOR FOR TODAY
Finish First
Don't smoke while you are doing something else. Finish up whatever you're doing and then you can light up.

The aim here is to just do one thing at a time, not to mix one with another. For example, if you normally smoke while having coffee, finish up your coffee without having a cigarette. Then smoke without drinking anything. If you find you don't need the cigarette then, because the trigger has been separated from it, just do some of the breathing exercises instead.

This kind of logic can be applied to other contexts, too. Let's say you normally smoke while chatting with a friend or while working. Just finish up first and *then* light up the cigarette you were going to have (if you must!). Have the chat, *then* the cigarette. Do the job, *then* have the cigarette. If you smoke on the phone, wait until you've come off the phone. You could keep a bottle of water by the phone and sip from that instead. If you smoke when you feel anxious, use the relaxation technique on page 130 instead of lighting up. Only allow yourself to smoke once you feel calm again. If you smoke while driving, pull over and stop, then get out of the car to smoke.

This technique allows you to smoke if you have to, but not necessarily when you normally would. You don't combine smoking with any other activity. This educates you only to smoke consciously and not because you've been cued to by an old association.

Caffeine

If you're a heavy caffeine user, it's worth bearing in mind that the effect of caffeine will double when you quit smoking, so consider switching to fruit juice now. It's also worth noting that coffee and nicotine are toxic partners when it comes to your health. A study in 2004 published in the *Journal of the American College of Cardiology* found that when people smoked and drank coffee at the same time, the combined effect on the arteries and blood flow was worse than the effects of the two substances added together. The study was carried out on healthy young people; the potential damage to the heart may be worse for older people or those with high blood pressure.

Day 9   Date: Jan 26th
YOUR TASK FOR TODAY

Cook something new

The goal of this task is to break your normal routines associated with preparing and eating a meal. We all have eating habits that have established themselves over the years, and often we eat without thinking, or resort to eating the things we've always had before. Just for today we want you to have something outside of your usual realm of gastronomic experience. You could be creative by just trying something simple or be really adventurous and try to cook something more advanced. Just make sure it's new, different and outside your normal comfort zone.

For example, have you ever made soup or bread from scratch? What about pancakes or hummus? How big a range of fruit and vegetables do you try? Ever had a dragon fruit, kiwi or lychee? What about fennel, celeriac or pak choi? Why not liven up some mash with spring onions, cheese or fresh herbs? Food will be even tastier when you stop smoking, so reconnect with the joy of food and start savouring some healthier alternatives from now on.

YOUR SMOKING-DISRUPTOR FOR TODAY
Change Places
Go to a different place whenever you are about to light up a cigarette.

Today you are going to move to another place before you light up. That means you'll do your smoking in a different location than the usual one. How does this work? Well, if you usually smoke at the table after eating, go into a *different* room or place to smoke. If you smoke after drinking a coffee, wash up your cup and *move* to a different place to smoke. Perhaps you tend to light up when socializing? Today if you feel like having a cigarette during a chat, you'll have to excuse yourself and go and smoke elsewhere.

This technique is breaking down the link between particular places and the urge to smoke. It builds on the changes you made earlier when you transformed your usual smoking location into a No-Smoking Zone. Places can be strong cues, and this technique separates the smoking from the place. Use it as much as you can from now on.

Day 10   Date: Jan 27th
YOUR TASK FOR TODAY

Take a different route

We all have places that we visit on a frequent basis, and regular routes that we know like the back of our hand. It might be our place of work, a friend's house or the local shops. Today when you make your usual trip to somewhere familiar, we want you to try to get there via a different route. Don't go the usual way. So perhaps drive a different way to work. Or if you always go by bus, get off one or two stops earlier and walk some of the way, trying a route you haven't been by before. Perhaps there's another way you can reach your local shops, or go somewhere different? Just inject a bit of variety into a frequent journey and you might be surprised how different things can be. Who knows what you'll see or whom you might meet? The novelty will wake up your brain, make it less passive.

YOUR SMOKING-DISRUPTOR FOR TODAY
Finish First *and* Change Places
Apply both of the disrupting techniques that you have learned, in combination. Finish what you are doing *and* move to a different place before you light up.

We are continuing to work at isolating your cigarette smoking as much as possible from the other things you do. Once again today don't combine the things you usually do – or the places you do them – with smoking.

For example, if you regularly have a morning coffee somewhere, make sure you finish that first before smoking and make sure you smoke in another PLACE. Remember, the idea is not to smoke at times or in situations where you normally would, but to separate them from each other as much as possible. Have a go and keep working on this separation technique to weaken those old associations.

Day 11   Date: Jan 28th
YOUR TASK FOR TODAY

A written pledge

This time we'd like you to sit down with pen and paper and just write for 15 minutes about all the reasons why you want to give up smoking. Express yourself any way you want. It can be in a few short notes, a letter to yourself or to a loved one. If you get stuck, the template on page 139 will help you. Write down why it is essential that you call it quits now. If it's for financial reasons, work out how much you'll save (a 20-a-day habit costs around £2,000 [$3,076 U.S.] a year). If it's health, count up the birthdays you want to have in the future and what you'd like to do on them (remember, one in two smokers dies early and loses about 16 years of life. Can you come up with 16 different birthday plans?).

You might like to list all the people who matter to you and convey all the ways you and your loved ones will benefit from your not smoking. Setting a good example to children is just one such reason. How many others can you think of?

If you're pregnant, why not write a letter to your unborn child? (You have a better chance of having a healthy baby as a non-smoker.) Perhaps you're diabetic or are going into hospital for an operation and have been told to try to give up smoking? Write about why that is critically important for your health now and in the future (by not smoking you will improve the rate at which wounds heal and also lower the risk of complications post-surgery, research from Sweden has shown).

You don't need to show anyone your letter, and you don't need to send it. Just keep this piece of paper somewhere that's safe and easy to remember. At later stages of the programme you are going to refer back to it as a reminder of why you're giving up, or even to bolster yourself if your resolve starts to wobble.

A PLEDGE

Now is the right time for me to quit smoking because:

I don't want to be a slave to nicotine anymore. I've smoked for 16 years and that's just too long.

I am doing this out of love for myself and love for the following people in my life:

Grandpa, Brendyn, Dad, Mama, Madi, Stephanie, BABA, everyone else I know and also the people that glare at me when I'm smoking.

By stopping smoking I will save around $ 50. per week. That is $ 200. per month or $ 2400. per year. WOW!

I will make good use of the money I save by

Giving back more, helping people out, saving money, and maybe more self-care.

By stopping smoking my health will improve in the following ways:

My skin will look better, my lungs will function better and exercise will be easier. Losing the addiction will improve my mental health.

And I look forward to being able to:

be around people smoking and not want a smoke, saving money, feel healthier, be freed from the addiction.

I am rejecting smoking because I know that life is a blessed joy and I want to live it to the full and have at least ..65........ *more birthdays. I also want to live to see*

the world come together instead of being so divided and become a better place.

YOUR SMOKING-DISRUPTOR FOR TODAY
Put It Aside
Do something else before you light up.

Here's another powerful technique to interrupt the automatic-ness of your smoking habit. Today, before you smoke, do something else first. At the very moment you get that yearning to light up, or find yourself blindly groping for your cigarettes, look around you and find something else to do. If you can't immediately spot anything, use one of the Habit-breaker Cards available at www.lovenotsmoking.com and do what it says on it.

Use this technique to put as much distance between the urge to smoke and the lighting up as possible. In between time, pick up the phone and ring a friend or relative. Put on some uplifting music. Polish your shoes, read the newspaper, wash your hands or clean your teeth. If you've finished eating and feel the urge to light up, get up and do the dishes first. Or pop outside and do some deep breathing. We've heard of people playing darts or taking up knitting to distract themselves. It doesn't matter what you do (within reason, of course) so long as you interrupt the connection between the urge to smoke and the actuality of putting flame to a cigarette.

With these techniques your brain is being subtly reprogrammed NOT to receive a hit of nicotine when it habitually anticipates one. Practise keeping this up as much as you can. Remember, when you don't succumb to the urge it *will* go away, probably in under two minutes. Just Do Something Different – and if you can make it pleasurable, even better. You may get so distracted by doing something different that you don't even have that cigarette anyway.

Day 12   Date: ..Jan.29th
YOUR TASK FOR TODAY

Rediscover childish fun

Do you remember what you did as a child for fun? How often these days do you really let go of your inhibitions and just allow yourself to 'play'? Today, try and rediscover the heady, carefree feeling that comes from just having fun. You don't have to see yourself as being 'childish' – more 'child-like' – as you release yourself a little from the grip, or habit, of being a 'sensible adult'. Your playful self is in there somewhere; it just needs coaxing out a little. Why not turn an everyday problem into a game and ramp up your pleasure quota at the same time?

Have you tried skipping or using a hula hoop since you were a child? When did you last lie on your back in the garden and watch the clouds or the stars? Have you thrown a Frisbee, had a pillow fight or kicked a ball around with friends lately? What about pond-dipping, tree-climbing, making a daisy chain or running down a hill? Anyone for bubble gum or a gobstopper? One habit into which most of us adults get is taking ourselves very seriously. Our 'fun' pathways in the brain withered and died from lack of use years ago. See if you can resurrect them. Experience that feeling of abandon, just for a short while, because play is an excellent problem-solver, an instant energizer and will lift your spirits.

YOUR SMOKING-DISRUPTOR FOR TODAY
Hold for Ten
Just wait ten minutes before you light up –
how hard can that be?

Today you're simply going to put ten minutes between wanting a cigarette and having one.

You'll disrupt the automatic habit of lighting up, and again tell your brain to wait. It can be done. YOU are the one who's in control now, not the nicotine master.

One technique you might like to try is: when you are about to smoke, stop and note the time on the clock. Then delay lighting up for as long as possible. Ten minutes should be the absolute minimum. Try setting the alarm on your phone or using an egg timer. It's not long to wait at all (especially now you know the craving only lasts a couple of minutes), and if you go and busy yourself doing something else, you'll hardly notice it passing. Whenever the urge creeps up on you, say to yourself, 'Just hang on a few minutes,' as you would to a persistent child. After ten minutes you may find the urge has passed and you don't light up at all. As you go through the day you may be able to delay for a little longer, 11 minutes then 12, as you realize the craving does subside and other things can intercede and fill the vacuum.

Sheila, 39: The first time I did this I grabbed an apple instead of a cigarette and made it last the full ten minutes. It was a really strange experience, eating it so slowly and dragging it out, chewing for ages. But I found I enjoyed every bite and it really calmed me down, too! Afterwards I felt much more relaxed; I couldn't remember the reason I'd reached for my cigarettes (someone had wound me up, I think) and then felt quite proud of myself so didn't even have that cigarette afterwards. I got through a load of apples when I was trying to give up, but kept telling myself it was better than smoking!

Day 13   Date: ...Jan 30th

YOUR TASK FOR TODAY

Socialize without smoking – at least once today

This Do Something Different task is a smoking-related one. And another habit-disruptor to break up those old associations. You might notice there are certain people around with whom you always smoke. They might be fellow smokers at work, mates down at the pub, particular family members or friends. Today we want you to resist the temptation to join in when others are having a smoke. In fact, whenever you do smoke it has to be on your own and never in the presence of others. The aim of this is to make smoking itself the focal behaviour, not to allow it to be associated with (and therefore reinforced by) pleasant socializing. And smoking alone, without your friends, will again make it a mindful, conscious activity and less automatic. You might even start to wonder why you're even bothering...

If you're single, you may find this has other unexpected social benefits, too. Research has found that non-smokers are more attractive to more of the population – so your romantic prospects could start looking up, too!

```
┌────────────────────────────────────────────┐
│     YOUR SMOKING-DISRUPTOR FOR TODAY         │
│            The Waiting Game                  │
│    Wait until something else happens first,  │
│       before you light that cigarette.       │
└────────────────────────────────────────────┘
```

Today's disruptor task is another delaying tactic (you're probably getting the hang of this by now!). So before you light up a cigarette, we want you to wait until something else happens first. If you're in the street or at a bus stop you can't light up until, say, an RV caravan has passed. Or a seagull has flown overhead. Or until you've heard a siren or seen a man wearing a baseball cap. You decide what it must be, but don't cheat by making it too easy.

If you're at home it might be that someone has to walk past the window first, or the washing cycle has to finish. At work it might be wait until a phone rings or you hear someone say the word 'customer', throw something in the trash or leave their desk. Whatever it is, it has to be something that doesn't happen every minute so that you're leaving things to chance.

While you are waiting you might be scanning the environment for your chosen sight, and that should refocus your mind. You may get so engrossed in people-watching, or in noticing the things going on around you, that you forget all about wanting to smoke. This task really does heighten your awareness of what goes on in you and around you, and, of course, it also interrupts the automatic-ness of smoking.

Many quitters have told us they found this technique to be very powerful in situations where they smoked as an emotional response or due to boredom. By tricking the mind into focusing on something else, you short-circuit the usual response.

Now have a peek at tomorrow's task, in case you need to reset your alarm for the morning.

Day 14   Date: Jan 31st
YOUR TASK FOR TODAY

Wake up earlier and prepare for quit day

We spend a lot of our lives asleep, and most of us have set times for getting up and going to bed. Like robots, we rigidly carry out our pre-programmed routines from the moment we get up. Our autopilot kicks in and we stagger from the bed to the shower to the breakfast table with our eyes barely open. Today we want you to switch from autopilot to driver and get up at least half an hour earlier. Use the extra time you have to disrupt your usual morning routine and do something different.

Since you are fast approaching your target quit day, this is a good time to get prepared and make sure you're ready. You might like to:

- Brush up on your relaxation technique
- Extend your No-Smoking Zone into other areas
- Stock up on some healthy snacks and fruit juices
- Remind your supporters that you're about to quit
- Review your written pledge to yourself

Choose Your Own Smoking-Disruptor for Today

Now you've got the hang of the Smoking-Disruptor Tasks, apply as many of them as you can today. Think about what has seemed to work best for you, which ones have really helped you see the connection between what you do and why you smoke. Put them into practice as much as you can today.

DISRUPTORS   CHECK WHICH
                             YOU WILL DO

FINISH FIRST   ☑

CHANGE PLACES   ☑

FINISH FIRST and   ☑
CHANGE PLACES

PUT IT ASIDE   ☑

HOLD FOR TEN   ☑

THE WAITING GAME   ☑

Week 3

YOUR FIRST NO-SMOKING WEEK

You've now arrived at your target quit-smoking date. From today onwards there is going to be **no smoking**. Not even a puff. No cutting down or switching to a 'light' brand. Neither of these works. You have to stop completely. The time to quit and start a new healthy life has arrived. Welcome it with open arms (ones without a cigarette at the end of them, please!).

Lots of smokers mistakenly think that brands described as 'light', 'low' or mild' are safer than ordinary ones. There is absolutely no evidence to support this. In fact, these products can force people to smoke more intensely to get the hit they need. They may also reduce the motivation to quit, and keep people smoking longer. In 2010 the US Food and Drug Administration sensibly banned the use of these names and replaced them with colours to differentiate one product from another without tricking people into thinking one brand was any less harmful than any other.

Over the past two weeks you've started to show your brain who's boss. Instead of jumping whenever it's commanded you with the signal 'SMOKE!' you've been strong enough to say, 'Hang on there a minute, I'm busy.' We like the ASH (Action on Smoking and Health) description of the smoking urge as 'a greedy parasite demanding constant attention'. He's not used to being disobeyed, but he's starting to quiet down a bit and is probably, already, you'll have noticed, learning to be less greedy and demanding. This week you are going to keep standing up to that greedy parasite by breaking habits and trying out different things, so we hope you've got the hang of how this works. Going without cigarettes from now on will be easier than you'd ever imagined. You've already started the process of breaking free; now you're making your one grand bid for freedom.

For starters, do make sure you've gotten rid of all your smoking paraphernalia. Dump ashtrays and throw away your last packet of cigarettes, lighter and matches. Don't forget to check pockets, drawers and handbags, too. Consign tobacco pouches, pipes, spittoons, papers, rollers, loose tobacco and cigarette cases to the trash. Don't just hide them; dispose of them for good. If it helps, have a bonfire to celebrate, wave to the refuse truck as it takes them away or organize a burial ceremony in the garden. Just make sure they're gone for good and there is absolutely no chance of them making a mysterious reappearance.

Dig out that written pledge about your decision to quit smoking, the one you produced on Day 11. Reread it and keep it with you at all times. Garner your army of supporters and get going.

What You Have to Do

- There is still a task for each day that you are on the Love Not Smoking: Do Something Different programme. Do the task you are set for that day. If you miss a day, carry on where you left off. The fewer days you miss, the better.
- It's time to make use of the DSD Habit-breaker Cards available at www.lovenotsmoking.com. Use these cards whenever you have the urge to light up a cigarette. They are there to help you whenever you feel a craving.

Withdrawal

Cold turkey. Withdrawal symptoms. Pangs. Deep cravings. These are all the things the smoker dreads when faced with quitting. People vary in the amount of withdrawal symptoms they get, and the type. If you know what to expect you can be prepared for it and also know that it will pass.

Some *light-headedness*, for example, is normal at first and sometimes experienced for the first 48 hours of quitting. If you experience this, just sit down and do some gentle breathing; it won't last more than half a minute or so.

You may also find that you experience some *night-time waking* or *mild insomnia* for the first week or so. Again, this is quite normal as your body is adjusting to ridding itself of nicotine. Keep some water by the bed and perhaps a book or a radio to tide you over until this symptom subsides.

Occasionally people find they suffer from *poor concentration* for the first two weeks after quitting. This isn't a serious problem or a sign that anything's wrong. Just keep a notebook handy if you feel you need extra help keeping on track.

For up to four weeks you may notice an increase in feelings of *irritability* or even *aggression*. Try to use some of the distractor exercises or the Habit-Breaker Cards to prevent overreacting while you are in this state. Ask for extra understanding from those around you, and reassure them you are doing all you can to get around this temporary issue.

Similarly you may find an increase in feelings of *depression* or *restlessness* in the first month. Make sure, if you are affected in this way, that you introduce as much exercise as possible into your daily routine to help deal with this. If you feel unable to cope, consult your GP rather than going back to smoking. You may need medication to help you through this period.

Because smoking has altered your body's metabolism, don't be surprised if you experience an *increase in appetite* when you quit. This can last for a couple of months as your body readjusts, but if you follow this programme closely you should find it helps you to resist the urge to overeat. You can also help yourself by making sure you have a nibble-box of healthy snacks on hand so you don't get tempted by high-calorie fillers.

> Please, please take note that the average craving only lasts a minute and a half. That's all. You are more than capable of getting through those 90 seconds. Remember the day you delayed for ten minutes at a time? Nobody died, did they?

The habit-breakers, disruptors and all the new things you're trying will make sure you navigate any minor period of discomfort easily. You may want to wear a watch or keep a check on the time from now on so that your brain doesn't distort the actual time. Use as many of the new techniques you've been adopting as you like, drinking fruit juice or deep breathing, or do a Habit-Breaker Card or two and then move on.

Cravings are annoying but they won't kill you. Unlike smoking. View the withdrawal symptoms as a positive sign. They are your body's way of telling you it is getting the nicotine bug out of your system. That's something to celebrate.

Research also tells us that, on average, a quitter gets no more than six episodes of craving a day, peaking on day three. Some say they peak again on day seven. That's probably when the significance of a week without smoking hits home. If this feels like cause for celebration, it certainly is. Celebration positively reinforces your new self-image and your achievement. Just watch out that your brain doesn't want to celebrate in the ways it's been conditioned to, with alcohol and a few cigs. Be proactive and plan another kind of treat for yourself. Spend time in the company of supportive friends and loved ones. Pamper or spoil yourself. You will have earned it.

Remember that the feelings of discomfort you are experiencing won't last forever. They will pass quickly and then you will never have to experience them again.

The DO SOMETHING DIFFERENT
Habit-Breaker Cards

At www.lovenotsmoking.com you'll find 50 DSD Habit-Breaker Cards. We suggest you print these, stick them onto card and cut them up so you have a 'pack' of cards. Keep them together as a set and have them on you at all times. Pop them in your pocket or handbag.

What Are the Habit-Breaker Cards?
Each card in the pack has a simple task specially designed to help you disrupt the way you are thinking and behaving. Hundreds of different habit-breakers have been trialed in studies, and the ones we have included on the website are those that have emerged as the most effective ones. We know they may seem a bit strange when you first look at them, but don't dismiss them. They could become your best allies in the fight against nicotine.

How Do I Use the Habit-Breaker Cards?
Any time you feel the urge to smoke, just take one of the cards at random and do what it says. Do it right away. If it's impossible in the situation you are in, try another.

Take the card out as soon as you feel the need to smoke or to combat a craving. Our research has shown they work well for heightened emotions, too, and can relieve stress and feelings of anxiety. Use them in response to any of your smoking triggers that still remind you of times when you would have lit up a cigarette. Trick the craving into subsiding. Do Something Different instead. The cards will give you some ideas, and you may find you adopt one or two that work really well for you, or even invent your own.

Just remember the craving is only an old habit creeping up on you. A craving lasts for less than two minutes. *It will subside if, instead of giving in to it, you start to behave in a different way.* You are using the cards to break the old connection between a smoking trigger and a smoking response. You recalibrate your thinking so that the smoking trigger becomes associated with a different action. This way the cravings get deflected. Psychologists sometimes call this 'competing response theory'. It's simple and very effective. The trigger gets met with a different response. Your DSD becomes the response that replaces smoking.

Most of the habit-breakers are adaptable to any situation in which you find yourself. However, there may be some that are just not possible to do at particular times. Of course you should use your own judgement and only ever use these cards when it is safe to do so. Don't endanger yourself or anybody else.

Medication

If you are on medication, while you were smoking you may have eliminated the drug at a faster rate than normal. Nicotine sometimes has this effect. So when you stop smoking it is possible that your body changes the way it handles your usual medication. Check with your GP as to whether, now you are a non-smoker, your medicine needs should be changed.

Day 15   Date: Feb 1st
YOUR TASK FOR TODAY

Rearrange the furniture

A huge proportion of what we think and do is the result of what's around us. Today, have a go at jumbling up some things in your immediate environment. This could be as simple as moving the furniture around, rearranging the pictures or swapping drawers around. It will give you the chance to try out new circulation routes at home or at work instead of the old ways to which you were used. Perhaps you could move your bed, or really shock the family and put the TV in a different place. Can the chairs be rearranged or your desk face a different direction?

The purpose of this seemingly random task is that rearranging your environment helps to disrupt well-learned action sequences that support habits. It challenges the brain to use different pathways. When you go to sit in a chair that's been moved, you'll be aware of how automatic and habit-driven much of your behaviour is. Notice how many times you go back to the old place and it will demonstrate to you how habitual many everyday routines are.

Now you've removed the ashtrays from your house, what other changes can you make to your domestic surroundings – and can you extend your No-Smoking Zone into new places?

**Get your free Habit-Breaker Cards
at www.lovenotsmoking.com.**
Use these cards whenever you have
the urge to light up a cigarette.

Time for a kiss or a close-up chat? Apart from breath, kissing a smoker can lead to an exchange of bad tastes and even the grains of ashes collected in the mouth. Yuk. At least all that is behind you now. After just a few hours without cigarettes your breath will begin to smell fresher. To whom are you going to pucker up?

Love Not Smoking Fact: By now your blood circulation will have returned to normal and your hands and feet will be warmer. After just eight hours of not smoking, your blood's nicotine and carbon monoxide levels will have halved and your oxygen levels returned to normal.

Day 16   Date: ..Feb..2nd..
YOUR TASK FOR TODAY

Do a good deed or random act of kindness

Today try to surprise someone with an unexpected, random act of kindness. And experience giving without expecting anything in return. Some things you might like to consider include:

- Help your neighbours by taking their trash cans in or mowing their lawn.
- Befriend some new colleagues; invite them for coffee or lunch.
- Do a small job for an elderly person or help with shopping.
- Pick up some litter.
- Leave a small gift on someone's desk or doorstep.
- Give others a lift or offer to take them home.
- Make someone a drink when they're too busy to stop.
- Read aloud to a child or elderly person.

Challenging all the things we take for granted is a useful way to gain fresh and different perspectives on our everyday lives. It also shows how a tiny effort can make a big difference. Yet sometimes, when we're cruising along on autopilot, we forget to make the effort to give something back. Have you registered as an organ donor, given blood or thought about volunteering? These are other ways of seeing the world as it is for others. A means of taking us outside of ourselves. And when you perform an act of kindness, studies have shown this 'catches on' and others are likely to spread generosity, too.

Ben and I once got caught in a heavy downpour of rain in Tokyo. A Japanese woman, spotting us two drowned British rats, approached us while carrying an umbrella. Then she promptly took another umbrella from her bag. She insisted we have it. It was such an unexpected but wonderful act of kindness. We've also heard of people who drop a few coins in a parking meter when time's nearly up, or pay for the next person's coffee at a drive-through, which creates an ongoing cascade of kindness. Warm frothy feelings all round.

Birju Pandya, an internet blogger who's made a habit of giving to others, describes the effect that acts of kindness have had on him:

> *I realize now that I've been literally rewiring my brain, that the consistent effort to do little things for others is what leads to making the larger acts of giving 'no-brainers'. What's more, this has led to a shift in perspective from being focused on results to being focused on the process. Don't expect the world to change, just give right now with no strings attached, and trust that the power of the act will continue the rewiring process in everyone involved.*

Join our Love Not Smoking support group today, at www.lovenotsmoking.com. Use this group for support if you are still getting the urge to light up a cigarette.

Have you said to anyone, 'No thank you, I don't smoke,' yet? If not, practise now how it feels to say it.

Ruby Rose

Love Not Smoking Fact: Smoking cessation has immediate health benefits. Within 24 hours of quitting, blood pressure and the chances of having a heart attack have already gone down. Carbon monoxide has been eliminated from your body and your lungs will already be starting to clear out smoking debris and phlegm/mucus.

Day 17   Date: Feb 5th
YOUR TASK FOR TODAY

Entertain yourself by doing something different

Your goal today is to find out about an alternative way of seeking entertainment for yourself. As a smoker you've got used to using a cigarette whenever you wanted a small treat or reward. Chances are, the more you did this, the less you sought out other ways of gaining pleasure. That's what we want you to do today. There are probably a host of fun and exciting things to do in your locality that you may not even be aware of. Why do we think of Saturday as a big night out? Do something different and make a Monday or Tuesday a big night. Or make lunchtime a time to do something special. Check your local newspaper or library for events listings. How about:

- Going swimming
- The cinema, either alone or with company
- A quiz night
- A dance class
- A music or sporting event
- Joining an amateur dramatics or a film club
- A moonlit walk
- Relaxing in the local library
- A picnic in the park
- Lunch with a friend
- Spending time in the country

Whatever you do, make sure it breaks the usual pattern of events and adds spice and variety to your life. Make a real and concerted effort to spend at least some of the day in a completely different environment, one that's free of your old habits and triggers. Did you know that even standing up changes the way our brain engages in certain types of thinking? So both small and large changes of environment can have a huge impact.

It's not too late to start using the Love Not Smoking app. Visit www.lovenotsmoking. com for details. Use the app if you still get the occasional craving when in a situation that reminds you of smoking.

Remember, to succeed at quitting you have to make firm plans and not leave things in life to chance. Boredom or too much time on your hands are your biggest enemies. Make sure you have plenty of new and different things arranged over the next few days. Give yourself assignments. Create a reading list. Write a memoir. File your photographs. If you don't shape your world, it will shape you, and sometimes in ways you don't want.

'Humans are producers of their life circumstance not just products of them.' – Albert Bandura

Love Not Smoking Fact: Already nicotine is no longer detectable in your body and you are starting to regain your sense of taste and smell. Perhaps you've already noticed that your sense of smell has improved as a result of not smoking? Allow this to heighten your awareness of nature, your environment, even the changes in the seasons. Maybe you've noticed again the smell of freshly cut grass? Or how good freshly baked bread smells? Your taste buds are awakening from their nicotine-induced sleep.

Day 18   Date: Feb 6th/22
YOUR TASK FOR TODAY

Go green today

Today, for the whole day, make it 'environment day' and see how much you can focus on being greener. When you ponder the wider issues about protecting your environment (and the devastating environmental impact of growing tobacco) or preserving the planet's resources, you are orienting your brain toward the importance of investing in the future. And giving up smoking is one huge step you have taken to invest in your own future. So this is an extension of that mindset. You can also celebrate the fact that you've stopped polluting your own environment and your own lungs.

What simple things can you change that would help the environment? For example:

- SAVE ENERGY – Turn lights off/switch to low-energy bulbs.
- SAVE WATER – Don't let taps leak or drip. Have showers, not baths.
- RECYCLE – Make an extra effort to sort and recycle your rubbish.
- DON'T DRIVE YOUR CAR – Walk or cycle, or use public transport.
- PLANT SOMETHING and create some oxygen.

If these are things you do normally, then think about adding something new. Perhaps explore ethical gift-buying or ethical holidays? Relax confidently in the knowledge that you are no longer supporting the tobacco companies. Go camping or do some gardening. Or just plant some seeds, indoors or out, to symbolize the big change you're making. Their growth will serve to remind you of your own personal growth as a result of giving up smoking. Even just making the effort to wear green or sit in a green room and reflect will focus the mind. The colour green is known to connect us with nature and instil a sense of harmony.

Get your free Habit-Breaker Cards at www.lovenotsmoking.com. Use these cards whenever your mind returns to those moments when you would light up a cigarette.

While you're noticing your environment, perhaps you've spotted how much fresher the air is around you now you're not smoking? Why not brighten up your table with a bunch of flowers where that ashtray used to be?

Love Not Smoking Fact: According to the 1998 UK Government White Paper *Smoking Kills*, within 72 hours of ceasing to smoke the bronchial tubes relax, making breathing easier and raising your energy levels. Enjoy that fresh, unpolluted air!

Day 19   Date: Feb 7th
YOUR TASK FOR TODAY

Time to learn something new

Today your task is to learn something new. Do you wonder how planes fly or how bees communicate with dance? As humans we were all born to learn. So nurture your curiosity and make a concerted effort today to pick up some new knowledge. If you don't feel a burning curiosity for a topic, just try something simple like learning a new word from the dictionary and dropping it into conversation. If you're feeling more adventurous, you could acquaint yourself with a new language or start swatting up on the constellations in the night sky. Look things up on the internet or in a dictionary or encyclopaedia. Browse in the library or a bookshop. Dust off that reference book on the shelf and discover the names of plants in your garden or the species of birds that visit. Away from nature, you could learn how to use a piece of technology that you own, finding out about all the unexplored options on your computer or mobile phone. Or sign up for an evening class or a college course. It's never too late to learn something new.

Everyone has a thirst for knowledge, but sometimes we get into the habit of not following through on our inner curiosity. Cultivating a love of learning will stimulate the mind and enrich every day of your life. It also stimulates brain growth and keeps neural connections in good condition. And the more interested you are in the world around you, the more interesting you'll become to others.

Never think you're too old to learn. Research shows that when the brain is kept in good shape, it will continue to build pathways that help you recognize patterns and see significance, and even solutions, much faster than a younger person.

Get your free Habit-Breaker Cards at www.lovenotsmoking.com. Use these cards whenever those old triggers sneak up on you.

Remember that keeping busy is critical in the early days of quitting. Your new task could be something you do with your hands if you still feel that something is missing. After all, as a smoker you were making hundreds of hand-to-mouth movements every day, and that will have become a habit. How about learning to juggle or getting a Rubik's cube or a yo-yo?

Love Not Smoking Fact: Speaking of hands, have you noticed how much better yours look and smell without the old traces of nicotine?

Day 20   Date: Feb 8th

YOUR TASK FOR TODAY

Get creative!

Today let your imagination loose on a creative pursuit. Creativity is about embracing the unknown and opening yourself up to it. It's about exploring things you've never seen, and ways of thinking that are alien to you. Draw, paint or sculpt anything that takes your fancy and do it without judgement – it doesn't have to be a masterpiece. Even if you don't know how to draw, just take a line for a walk on a blank piece of paper – make some marks or doodle. Or try to recreate an image from your memory of a place, a face or something totally abstract. Don't judge the result because perfectionism is the enemy of creativity. Just focus on having fun and opening your mind. Once you're engrossed you'll get into a complete state of flow and won't notice time passing. You could experiment with drawing left-handed and experience a different sensation when pencil connects with paper or the image on the page disconnects from the one in your mind. Creativity is all about relinquishing past ways of thinking, and this is exactly what you have done by letting go of the need to smoke. Being curious, willing to take risks and expressing yourself in an entirely different way will also help to set you free from your old ways.

Join our Love Not Smoking support group today, at www.lovenotsmoking.com, for whenever you need support to disrupt an old behavioural pattern.

If you've been putting aside the money you normally spend on cigarettes, this is a good time to treat yourself to a reward for having gone five days without one. The average health benefit of quitting amounts to five extra years of life, so that may be reward in itself. Celebrate the start of your healthy lifestyle.

Love Not Smoking Fact: One study, involving US naval female workers and published in *Tobacco Control*, found that non-smokers earn significantly more than smokers. So things might be looking up for you financially in a number of ways. As well as counting the money you've saved by not smoking, you may find the confidence now to ask for a pay raise or move to a better-paid job.

Day 21   Date: Feb 9th
YOUR TASK FOR TODAY

Do Something Different to pamper yourself a little

Now you've stopped smoking, your attitude to quitting will play a huge part in determining how successful you are. If you see it as an act of self-deprivation and feel sorry for yourself, you're going down the wrong road. By quitting you have given yourself a huge gift, possibly years of better health and longer life. So today give yourself a treat to celebrate this gift to your future self. Reward your present self today. You might choose to go back to bed with a cup of tea and the newspaper, have a long soak in the bath, a nap in the sun, a foot soak or back scrub. Why not watch your favourite movie or buy a glossy magazine or special chocolate? How about booking a manicure now your hands are free from the taint of smoke, or treating yourself to an aromatherapy massage? Whatever you decide to do, remind yourself that you've earned this treat for kicking the nicotine habit.

Get your free Habit-Breaker Cards at www.lovenotsmoking.com. Use these cards if you still get the odd craving.

As you get dressed today, notice how your clothes are becoming smoke-free and losing that stale cigarette smell. If any still have the remnants of old smoke lingering on them, hang them out in the fresh air, buy some fabric freshener – or take a trip to the dry cleaner's.

Week 4

NEW BEHAVIOURS

Welcome to Week 4, your second week of not smoking. You're going to continue the reprogramming that you've begun. You'll carry on nudging those brain neurons in a different direction. This will help to make sure that those old habits and associations have taken a back seat. If you've been doing something different at least every day by now, you should be immensely proud of how far you've come. And we hope you're feeling revitalized and excited about your future.

For the next part of the programme you're going to expand your personality. More specifically, you are going to increase your behavioural repertoire by adding some new behaviours. Why? Because enhanced behavioural flexibility is an important antidote to old, habitual ways of thinking and behaving. It will mean you have new, positive habits to replace some of those you've ditched. You'll build up your reserves of positive antidote activities to help you cope with whatever life throws at you.

This week you will be building on the great work you've been doing so far and extending it from your behaviour more into your personality. You have seven new behaviours to try – one for each day. The aim is to expand your behaviours in several different areas. Not only are you breaking down old connections, the ones that triggered smoking, but you will be building up new ones in their place to keep you smoke-free.

Without realizing it, you will have established a relatively fixed and limited range of responses for every situation that comes your way. As we have said before, the brain is a habit machine and operates on the efficiency principle. So if something has worked before, it will default to using it again rather than putting in the extra effort needed to come up with a new response. Unfortunately, though, this can lead to a complete shutting down of some aspects of the personality. As a result, our world can shrink.

This week we're going to bring all those possible responses back into the open. If you are prepared to risk trying something new, in terms of your responses to situations and people, you might be pleasantly surprised to find you get something different back. You are enhancing your behavioural flexibility. It has been said that 'people who are wrapped up in themselves make very small packages'. We want you to be a larger package from now on!

Our research has demonstrated that being a more flexible person, with the ability to behave in varied rather than fixed ways, makes a difference to other areas of life and the ability to both cope with, and sustain, change. A person who functions well in the world – and that includes being free from addictions – has at their disposal skills and abilities that are well matched to what life asks of them. That's why this programme stresses the importance of being versatile and adaptable. We really do believe that your ability to 'flex' your personality is the best buffer against any problems, setbacks or stressors you might encounter in your life. It gives you a rich bank of personal resources that are compatible with the demands placed upon you, or ones against which you might come up. And as you continue to transform yourself, your confidence will grow, too, along with your belief in your personal power to change.

The areas of behaviour that we are going to work on developing are derived from FIT Science, which Ben founded about 20 years ago. If you want to read more about the background to FIT Science, we go into it more in Week 6. For now, though, we just want you to think about which aspects of your personality you automatically call upon as you go about your daily life. And we're going to focus in particular on the following behaviours:

- Unassertive – Assertive
- Individually-centered – Group-centered
- Calm/Relaxed – Energetic/Driven
- Definite – Flexible
- Spontaneous – Systematic
- Introverted – Extroverted
- Conventional – Unconventional

In the list above, each of the behaviours has a partner, but neither of the pair is good or bad. It depends on the situation in which they are used. Your goal is not to use only one of the pair consistently, but to be able to use both as the situation demands. To develop this behavioural flexibility we want you to try ways of behaving that you might not naturally use. That means being willing to play with ideas, tinker with thoughts, and bend and stretch your personality to see how it could serve you better.

Many of us have a tendency to behave in the same way in a given situation. The idea this week is to see what happens when you experiment with behaving in the opposite way to usual – when you try to do what *doesn't* come naturally. You don't have to become a different person overnight, but just begin playing with slightly different traits. That doesn't mean you totally abandon your existing strengths, but you do start to become aware of when they do and don't work to your advantage. You may find the reactions and feelings you have are quite different. You might notice that, in certain situations, your non-usual behaviour actually works well and is better. With a wider repertoire of behaviours you might find you are less likely to be habitual, and less likely to need to smoke.

This week we encourage you to take some time to study yourself and your habitual behaviours and reactions. For example, do you really want to go to the pub after work, or are you just going to please everyone else? Are you attached to a strongly held opinion because it's what you feel or because you don't want to lose face? Do you dress the way you do because you love it and it expresses your individuality – or just because it's what people expect of you? This week test out how it feels to break out of the mould you've set yourself.

An important point: when you try a different behaviour you must be sure that it is appropriate to the situation and that it will not hurt you or anybody else.

Get your free Habit-Breaker Cards at www.lovenotsmoking.com. Use these cards whenever you have the urge to light up a cigarette. Remember, a craving will subside within two minutes.

Day 22   Date: Feb 10th
YOUR TASK FOR TODAY

Are you unassertive or assertive?

These are two very different ways of reacting in a situation.

- **Assertive:** insisting upon your rights, or asking for what you want
- **Unassertive:** not putting yourself forward, not asking for what you want.

How Do You Rate Yourself?

Place a check on the scale below:

Do you usually behave in an ASSERTIVE or UNASSERTIVE manner?	5	4	3	2	1	0	1	2	3	4	5
	☑	☐	☐	☐	☐	☐	☐	☐	☐	☐	☐
	Unassertive				Neither one nor the other				Assertive		

Consistently being too much one way or the other is not a good thing, because there will be times when either one or the other behaviour is more appropriate. So, for example:

- Consistently being assertive could make you appear aggressive or failing to take account of others.
- Being too unassertive might mean you never get what you want or that you let others make decisions for you.

But there are varying degrees of assertiveness/ unassertiveness in between. These may be acceptable alternative ways for you to behave, and today we ask you to consider *doing something different*.

Today's Task

During the course of the day situations will arise when you would normally react assertively or unassertively. Try to anticipate some of these situations. Think about when they might happen and how you would normally react in terms of assertiveness/unassertiveness. For example, perhaps you always take charge in meetings or with your family? Are you always first to air your views on whatever is being discussed? Today, even if it's just for a short period of time, try sitting back and being unassertive. And then just observe what happens.

So, if you're normally assertive, here are a few thoughts about how you might behave differently today:

To Be More Unassertive	I'll Try
Stay in the background more.	☐
Ignore criticism, don't react.	☐
Behave as if another person knows better than you.	☐
Let somebody else decide or choose for you.	☐
(or think of your own): _____	☐

Or maybe you are generally an unassertive person? Today you could try being more confident and direct with someone. Express yourself with enthusiasm and confidence. Step forward, smile and don't hold back. Say NO and mean it.

So, if you're normally unassertive, here are a few thoughts :

To Be More Assertive	I'll Try To
Speak up when you would normally hold back.	☐
Be direct in asking for what you want.	☐
Express an opinion.	☐
Be more forceful in putting something across you believe in.	☐
Say NO (when it's OK to).	☐
(or think of your own): _____	☐

Get your free Habit-Breaker Cards at www.lovenotsmoking.com. Use these cards whenever you feel old habits threatening to take you over or you are tempted to revisit old choices.

Day 23   Date: Feb 11th
YOUR TASK FOR TODAY

Are you individually-centered or group-centered?

- **Group-centered**: taking a team view, going along with the group
- **Individually-centered**: doing your own thing, going against the crowd.

As humans, we all belong to many different 'groups'. These might, for example, be our work colleagues, club members, friends, team-mates or family members. At certain times in our lives, often daily, situations arise when we have to consider our own view and behaviour in relation to one or more of these other groups of people. Today, try to think about when you might find yourself in one of these group situations. When faced with these situations, some people take a more individual view, whereas others may take more account of the group as a whole. Again, being too much one way isn't a good thing.

- Being too individually-centered might make you appear selfish and inconsiderate of others.
- Being too group-centered might mean that you don't do what's best for you or for the other groups to which you belong.

But it's still possible to try different ways of being slightly more or less group/individually-centered and these can be alternative ways for you to behave differently.

How Do You Rate Yourself?

Place a check on the scale below:

Do you usually behave in an INDIVIDUALLY- or GROUP-CENTERED manner?	5	4	3	2	1	0	1	2	3	4	5
	☐	☐	☑	☐	☐	☐	☐	☐	☐	☐	☐
	Individually-centered					Neither one nor the other			Group-centered		

Today's Task

During the course of today, notice situations when you would normally be more group-centered or more individually-centered. Try to anticipate some of these situations and behave in a different way. Think about when they might happen and how you would normally react in terms of being group- or individually-centered. For example, perhaps you are more of a group-centered person and naturally give priority to the immediate needs of the group (this could be your colleagues, family, team-mates, etc.)? People often are group-centered because it's the easy option – but actually, sometimes an individually-centered approach can benefit the group even more in the long run.

Group-centered people, while being great team-players, may also be driven by worrying about what others think of them. This gets in the way of doing the right thing. And focusing on what others think is a huge distraction from the things in life that are really important. If you feel good about life, does it really matter whether that other person approves of you?

Today, even if it's just for a short period of time, why not try the following:

To Be More Individually-Centered	I'll Try To
Take an individual stance when it's appropriate to do so.	☐
Share your individual needs with one or more members of the group.	☐
Do the right thing without asking others.	☐
Do something purely for yourself.	☐
(or think of your own): _____	☐

Or maybe you are generally an individually-centered person? This may mean that you're good at getting what you want from life and don't get distracted by the demands of other people or worry too much about what others think of you. There are real advantages to be had from being this way, but in some circumstances taking account of others is essential, too.

Today you could try being more group-focused; for example, you might:

To Be More Group-Centered	I'll Try To
Ask other group members what you can do for the group.	☑
Offer support or help to another group member.	☐
Initiate a chat with one or more of your group about the needs of the group.	☐
Organize something in which all the group can take part	☐

Be willing to learn from family and friends; try to remain open to the suggestions of others. ☑

(or think of your own): _____ ☐

Get your free Habit-Breaker Cards at www.lovenotsmoking.com. They can still be useful for interrupting the automatic behaviours we all fall foul of now and again.

While thinking about your social group, consider how many of your friends would rather you didn't smoke in their cars or their homes, and how being a non-smoker means you'll feel less of a social outcast. Talk to people who've kicked the habit too, and remember to surround yourself with supporters, those who are willing you to quit for good.

Day 24   Date: Feb. 12th
YOUR TASK FOR TODAY

Are you calm and relaxed?
Or energetic and driven?

- **Calm/Relaxed**: being peaceful, not stressed; without tension
- **Energetic/Driven**: enthusiastic, motivated

People vary in the extent to which they are calm or energetic, and this not only varies according to personality but also according to situations and even the time of day. Some people, however, may always be too relaxed in the way they approach things, while others seem to be permanently hyper. How does this apply to you? There will be benefits from being different from the way you normally are in some situations. For example:

- Being too relaxed and calm might sometimes make you appear lazy and not interested in what's going on.
- Being too energetic and driven might mean there are times when you miss opportunities because you're going too fast and not reflecting on what you are doing.

How Do You Rate Yourself?

Do you usually behave in a CALM/RELAXED or ENERGETIC/ DRIVEN manner?	5	4	3	2	1	0	1	2	3	4	5
	☐	☑	☐	☐	☐	☐	☐	☐	☐	☐	☐
	Calm/Relaxed					Neither one nor the other			Energetic/Driven		

Today's Task

Today, Try to Take a Different Perspective!

For example, if you're normally energetic you could try and adopt a more relaxed approach to life today. Perhaps your energetic nature makes you feel stressed, or you worry too much at times? What if you felt there were nothing you could control in the world except for your own feelings, thoughts and actions? If you accepted that everything else was out of your hands, would you worry less about things over which you have no control?

To Be More Calm and Relaxed	I'll Try To
Take five minutes' time out to just think, once an hour, every hour.	☐
Do something really slowly instead of rushing through it.	☐
Put something off until later.	☐
Let go, of others and the outside world, and focus only on things you *can* control.	☐
Let yourself be bored – don't fight it.	☐
(or think of your own): _____	☐

Or maybe you are generally a calm and relaxed person? Today you should try being more energetic and driven; for example, you might:

To Be More Energetic and Driven	I'll Try To
Take on a new role or activity.	☑
Take 20 per cent less time over everything you do.	☑
Do something you've been putting off for a long while.	☑

Take some initiative when you'd normally leave it to somebody else. ☑

Exercise first thing in the morning to raise your energy levels. ☑

(or think of your own): _____ ☐

Get your free Habit-Breaker Cards at www.lovenotsmoking.com. They can have all sorts of uses when you need a way of putting a stop to unwanted thoughts or behaviours.

Love Not Smoking Fact: By now the average quitter is said to have only one or two episodes of craving per day, so you may find you need the Habit-Breaker Cards less. But don't forget some of the tricks you've learned to liberate yourself from old habits.

Day 25   Date: Feb.14th
YOUR TASK FOR TODAY

Are you definite or flexible?

- **Definite**: certain, sure, decisive
- **Flexible**: open to change, willing and able to adapt.

People think flexibility is a good thing. When an unforeseen event happens, you have to be able to switch tacks. But there are times when wobbling around just won't do and you need to make a decision. Similarly, having definite ideas about what you want and what you are trying to achieve makes it more likely to happen, but that doesn't mean you don't remain open to better suggestions. So there are both pros and cons with each of these ways of behaving. But if you have a tendency to behave in just one of the ways, you could be missing out on all sorts of opportunities. Also:

- Being too flexible might mean that you lack focus and are too easily diverted from what you want or need.
- Being too definite can make you appear insensitive to the needs and views of others, and give them the wrong impression of you.

184

How Do You Rate Yourself?
Place a check on the scale below:

Do you usually	5	4	3	2	1	0	1	2	3	4	5
behave in a	☐	☐	☐	☐	☐	☐	☐	☐	☐	☑	☐
DEFINITE or											
FLEXIBLE	Definite				Neither one					Flexible	
manner?					nor the other						

Today's Task

Today, have a go at being different. Once again, the aim of this is to get you to explore and expand your behavioural repertoire and minimize the chances of those old habits returning. For example, if you're normally flexible you could experiment with being more definite today:

To Be More Definite	I'll Try To
Take a stance and see the benefits of a firm line.	☑
Don't be so accommodating (only when you think it is appropriate).	☑
Make a strategic decision and act on it, unswayed by the immediate circumstances you are in.	☑
Pay more attention to the big issues, and don't get distracted by the smaller details of a situation.	☑
Stick to a choice and don't change your mind	☑
(or think of your own): _____	☐

Maybe you are generally very definite and have strong views? When did you last critically reflect on some of the assumptions you've acquired? Think about how willing you would be to let go of some of them. Today, try being more flexible in your approach:

To Be More Flexible	I'll Try To
Let someone sell you something small you'd already decided against.	☐
Imagine you are on the receiving end of something you do and ASK – how does it seem from the other person's point of view? This might be something as simple as how you interact at the supermarket check-out, or how you reply to an issue your partner raises.	☐
On the hour, each hour, stop before you do what you are naturally going to do next. Could you try something different that might be more beneficial?	☐
Try someone else's suggestion instead of your own.	☐
Let others be 'right' today; don't criticize.	☐
Listen to the views of someone with whom you disagree and suspend judgement.	☐
(or think of your own): _____	☐

Get your free Habit-Breaker Cards at www.lovenotsmoking.com. Use these cards whenever you feel the need to interrupt your habitual response to a situation.

Love Not Smoking Fact: Remember, since stopping smoking, your heart and lung function have already begun to improve considerably. You might notice you're less breathless when you run for the bus or exercise, or you may find going upstairs easier. If you could wear your lungs on the outside they'd already be starting to look much nicer than they did before!

Day 26   Date: Feb. 18th / 22
YOUR TASK FOR TODAY

Are you spontaneous or systematic?

- **Spontaneous**: doing things on the spur of the moment
- **Systematic**: planning and considering in advance; orderly.

Some people are more spontaneous than others, with a tendency to do things on the spur of the moment, seemingly without giving them much thought. Then there are the more systematic folk who think every step through really carefully before acting. You probably know where your natural tendency lies. Are you more spontaneous or more systematic? Whichever it is, today you can try being different to the way you normally are. As always, it's not necessarily good to be too much one way or the other. The situation should decide.

- Being too spontaneous might mean you act too hastily and make mistakes.
- Being too systematic might mean you don't make the most of a situation and miss out on opportunities.

How Do You Rate Yourself?

Place a check on the scale below:

Do you usually behave in a SPONTANEOUS or SYSTEMATIC manner?	5	4	3	2	1	0	1	2	3	4	5
	☐	☐	☐	☑	☐	☐	☐	☐	☐	☐	☐
	Spontaneous				Neither one nor the other				Systematic		

Today's Task

Today, look for an opportunity to experiment with a different approach. If you're normally spontaneous you could try adopting a more systematic approach to one or two situations that arise during the course of the day:

To Be More Systematic	I'll Try To
Make plans now for something that's going to happen some time in the future.	☑
Organize an area of your life that's too haphazard – anything from sorting out your CDs to putting your finances in order.	☑
Make a list of the things you want to achieve in the next week, next year and in your life. Add some notes on how you want to reach these goals and the steps you will take.	☑
Timetable your whole day in half-hour slots.	☑
(or think of your own): _____	☐

Maybe you are usually systematic in the way you go about things? Today you could try being more spontaneous:

To Be More Spontaneous	I'll Try To
Do something on the spur of the moment.	☐
Ignore your plans and just do what feels right.	☐
Try something silly or frivolous – just for fun.	☐
Phone up an old friend out of the blue.	☐
Let the day unfold without organizing it; just see what happens.	☐
(or think of your own): _____	☐

It's not too late to start using the Love Not Smoking app. Visit www.lovenotsmoking .com for details. Use it whenever you feel you need to.

Try to keep in mind the importance of doing new things, being open to new ideas and relishing the new opportunities that come your way.

Love Not Smoking Fact: You may feel you have life more under control since you quit. A study from the University of Iowa, published in the *Journal of Studies on Alcohol and Drugs*, showed that non-smokers scored higher than smokers on tests of ability to reason, plan and organize.

Day 27   Date: ...February 19th...
YOUR TASK FOR TODAY

Are you introverted or extroverted?

- **Introverted**: inward-looking, not outgoing
- **Extroverted**: outgoing, sociable

People vary in terms of how naturally outgoing they are. You probably have an idea of whether you are more of an introvert or an extrovert, although there's no rule that says you can only be one or the other. Today we want you to experiment with acting in the opposite way to how you normally would, and once again to dabble outside your natural tendency. Remember, the idea is to try out different ways of behaving, especially if you have a tendency to be pretty predictable. As well as trapping you in your habits, always behaving in the same way has other downsides:

- Consistently being too extroverted might make some people think you are too cocky or overconfident. Even though you may think you're the life and soul of the party, this can put some people off you and may prevent you from developing positive, enduring relationships with others.
- Being too introverted might mean you don't give people the chance to get to know you. They may not even be aware of your strengths and may underestimate or overlook you.

How Do You Rate Yourself?

Place a check on the scale below:

Do you usually	5	4	3	2	1	0	1	2	3	4	5
behave in an EXTROVERTED	☐	☐	☐	☐	☐	☐	☐	☐	☑	☐	☐
or INTROVERTED manner?	Extroverted				Neither one nor the other					Introverted	

Today's Task

Today, experiment a little with being a different person. Just for the day, or on one occasion, try out how it feels to be the opposite to how you would normally be.

For example, if you think you are an introvert, today you could try to:

To Be More Extroverted	I'll Try To
Contribute to a discussion when you wouldn't normally express your opinion. Speak up and make yourself heard.	☑
Make the first move in a friendship situation, e.g. plan a party or organize a get-together with friends.	☑
Get out of your shell, e.g. by talking to somebody new or somebody you meet at an event.	☑
Be more outgoing and draw attention to yourself, perhaps by telling a funny story or letting people know your views.	☑
(or think of your own): _____	☐

Or maybe you are more of an extrovert? Today you could try being more introverted:

To Be More Introverted	I'll Try To
Listen more and speak less.	☐
Spend some time alone, enjoying your own company when you would not normally.	☐
Say no to a social invitation.	☐
Let yourself fade into the background a bit more.	☐
Don't interrupt other people or finish their sentences.	☐
(or think of your own): _____	☐

Get your free Habit-Breaker Cards at www.lovenotsmoking.com. Use these cards whenever you feel your old tendencies trying to get a grip on you.

Reflect on the new person you've become as a non-smoker. You might want to record your success with an inspiring painting or photograph; choose one that will encourage daily motivation. Remember, too, that fewer cigarettes equals more birthdays ... how will you celebrate?

Day 28   Date: Feb 21st
YOUR TASK FOR TODAY

Are you conventional or unconventional?

These are two opposite ways of behaving:

- **Conventional** means traditional, formal, behaving according to normal custom and generally 'fitting in'
- **Unconventional** means being different and willing to stand out from the crowd.

During the course of the day, situations will arise when you would react in a way most people would, especially if you are a conventional person. Try to anticipate some of these situations. Think about when they might happen and how you would normally react in terms of being conventional or unconventional.

Too much of either of these is not necessarily a good thing, as it could mean you're lopsided rather than having a healthy balance of both behaviours. Indeed:

- Being too conventional could make you appear formal, staid and inflexible. How would it feel to let go of your image of yourself, just for a short while? Can you allow yourself to break the odd rule or ignore convention now and again?
- Being too unconventional might mean you don't fit in or you stay outside the group and people may find it hard to relate to you. Do you deliberately go against the tide? There may be times when being that way means you don't get the best from situations or relationships.

How Do You Rate Yourself?
Place a check on the scale below:

Do you usu-ally behave in an UNCONVENTIONAL or CONVENTIONAL manner?	5	4	3	2	1	0	1	2	3	4	5
	☐	☐	☑	☐	☐	☐	☐	☐	☐	☐	☐
	Unconventional				Neither one nor the other				Conventional		

There are varying degrees of conventional/unconventional. These may be acceptable alternative ways for you to behave, and today we ask you to consider doing something different.

Today's Task

During the course of the day, see if situations arise when you would normally react conventionally or unconventionally, although most people err on the conventional side. Try to anticipate some of the situations when you can react and behave in a different way. Think about when they might happen and how you would normally react in terms of conventionality. For example, perhaps you are an unconventional person in some areas and naturally resist going with the crowd? Today, even if it's just for a short period of time, why not try to fit in a little?

To Be More Conventional	I'll Try To
Make the more conventional choice rather than having to be different.	☐
Consider the more traditional alternative.	☐
Conform and take the easily acceptable option.	☐

Agree with someone even if you don't share their view. ☐

(or think of your own): _____ ☐

Maybe you are generally a conventional person? Habit-breaking may be achieved more easily if you try being more unconventional. Why not go Christmas shopping in July or have a barbecue in winter? So, if you're normally conventional, today why not break a small rule of your own making?

To Be More Unconventional	I'll Try To
Look at situations from a completely different angle, e.g. as a teenager/a foreigner or an alien might.	☐
Wear something different and daring.	☑
Take something in your life that's very ordinary and change it, e.g. your voicemail message, choice of food or décor.	☑
Look at what others are doing and be different.	☑
Voice a radical opinion or reshape standard practice.	☐
(or think of your own): _____	☐

**Get your free Habit-Breaker Cards at
www.lovenotsmoking.com.** Use these
cards whenever you need to interrupt
a habitual behaviour or thought.

Have you smartened up your wardrobe since you've become a non-smoker? Is it time to get a more adventurous image? Are you finding you have more energy, look better and smell fresher since you quit?

DSD Boredom-Busters

Boredom is one of the quitter's biggest danger traps. Eight out of ten of our smokers told us they smoked mostly when they were bored. The good news is you don't have to be bored. But you *do* have to have lots of things to do whenever you find yourself at a loose end. That's why we've compiled this list of all the things our quitters have told us they do to keep from being bored and to make sure they keep doing something different.

- Clean shoes
- Put all my photos into albums
- Organize my CDs
- Clean the car
- Research my family tree
- Pull up weeds
- Learn t'ai chi
- Organize my make-up and throw out old stuff
- Make herbal tea
- Play with the children
- Make my own birthday cards
- Dance with my wife/husband
- Go for a bike ride
- Join my library
- Clean out my fridge
- Organize my email
- Update my address book
- Clean up the garage
- Give away stuff I don't need
- Back up my computer
- Start a recipe book
- Take photos of a walk I took
- Try roller-skating

- Make the best ever hot chocolate
- Pick up litter or rubbish
- Make my own ice cream
- Run or walk briskly
- Arrange flowers
- Watch my favourite film
- Play on the Wii
- Have a power nap
- Play with a ball
- Knit or sew
- Practise a foreign language
- Sing really loudly
- Play snooker or pool
- Watch birds
- Have a bonfire
- Update my CV
- Make a playlist of my favourite songs
- Cook with a new ingredient
- Swim underwater
- Make up a quiz
- Play in a sports tournament
- Join a dating website
- Make photo-portraits of the family
- Build an indoor garden
- Sign up for a course
- Sit as a model for an artist
- Listen to audiobooks
- Go beachcombing
- Fix something that's broken
- Sign up for learning a computer program
- Go to the gym
- Sell something on eBay
- Learn first aid
- Have a game of cards
- Become a volunteer

Week 5

CHANGING WHAT YOU DO

Welcome to your third week of not smoking, and congratulations on getting this far. You and your loved ones must be hugely proud of what you've accomplished to date. You'll have noticed how much better life is beginning to feel, as you regain your sense of taste and smell, and your energy levels improve. Within two weeks of quitting there is a general improvement in your body's circulation, so you may already be finding that walking is easier and you don't get out of breath so quickly.

Speaking of walking, are you one of those people who avoids stepping on cracks in the pavement? In the film *As Good As It Gets*, Jack Nicholson's character, Melvin Udall, is a man of many strange habits. His medicine cabinet is rammed full of orderly stacks of soap. That's because whenever he uses a bar of soap, he throws it away afterwards. On leaving his apartment he closes his door several times and counts how many times he has done it. Once outside he avoids all cracks on the pavement. He eats at the same restaurant, sits at the same table, insults anyone who is at his table to make them leave, and insists that the same waitress, Carol, serve him. He taps his slippers three times before putting them on. The strict manner with which his habits rule his life makes for a hilarious film, especially when he is asked to look after a neighbour's dog and this threatens to make his obsessive behaviours unmanageable. Perhaps the funniest part is when the dog starts to avoid stepping on the pavement cracks.

OK, Melvin Udall clearly suffers from an obsessive compulsive disorder. He's an extreme case. His overwhelming need to carry out his compulsive acts is hugely disabling and makes his life at best difficult and at worst sometimes unbearable.

But stop and think for a moment. Don't we all have these tendencies in a milder way? Do you have a favourite coffee mug and get a bit miffed if a guest inadvertently uses it? Do you have 'your' side of the bed? Do you try to get the same seat on the train, the same locker at the gym, the same table in the cafeteria or the same spot in the parking lot? Do you do things in a certain order, always read the paper from the back, have to position things symmetrically or put a little bit of everything on your fork? We know an elderly woman who still doesn't completely drain her teacup, even though she hasn't used leaf tea for over 30 years. We all have an affinity with repetition and habit, often when there's no good reason for it. It's just familiarity, our comfort zone.

When I (Karen) was about seven, we went on a family holiday to Italy. By coach. It was very memorable for a number of reasons, mainly to do with nausea, but most notably because halfway through the journey we had to switch coaches. My father decided to try positioning us in different seats (none were pre-booked) on the replacement coach. His vain hope was that this would quell the tendency of my brother and me to vomit every time the coach navigated a bend in the road. As we took our new seats there was an uproar among the other travellers. Most of them were aghast at the prospect of not being able to sit in the same seats they had had for the previous two days (it was a long trip), even though you might think they too would have welcomed a switch around. People are often resistant to change for no good reason.

Do you recognize yourself here? Like all of us, you probably have a few routines or set ways into which you've slipped without even noticing. So this week you are going to continue to shake up the regularity of your life. This will keep things fresh, banish more habits and push you to experience things a bit differently. So far in the programme you've been trying to do new things and to behave in ways that you wouldn't normally. That's been working to break down old connections, remove all the old smoking triggers and associations, and give you an expanded repertoire of behaviours.

This week we're going to turn the spotlight more onto your own personal habits. You will have all kinds of automatic behaviours, personal preferences and routines that you probably aren't even aware of – everybody has. Because that's what habits are – *action without thought*.

This week we're going to help you gain some self-insight and identify some of these. Bring them out into the open and hold them up to scrutiny. Then, each day, you're going to try something a bit different. Something that's just outside your comfort zone and will expand you as a person. If that sounds a bit scary, remember it's natural to feel that way – but also remind yourself of how far you have come. Dorothy Rowe, in her *Guide to Life*, points out that, 'If you try to make everything in your life secure, what you gain in security you lose in freedom.' So, are you ready for a bit of habit-spotting? Here we go!

What Are Habits?

Your habits are your natural tendencies, the way you would normally behave if you didn't stop and think about it. The old well-worn pathways in your brain. They might include:

- Automatic or unconscious reactions
- Set routines you follow regularly
- Things you do without thinking
- Unanalyzed views and beliefs
- Predictable or automatic responses

As humans, we are all habit machines. That's because what's automatic is an effective method of simplifying a complex world. Every second the brain receives around 10 to 12 million bits of information to process; way too much even for as sophisticated a piece of kit as the human brain. So we have automatic processes, or habits, to enable us to make sense of all this information without having to process it all consciously (we can only consciously process around 50 bits/second). The brain effectively selects or filters the incoming information using these automatic processes. It operates on a need-to-know basis, and most of the time it does not need to know. So, habits take over – they define us.

Consequently, a lot of information-processing and decision-making become automated by these (unconscious) filters. The efficient brain defaults to processing new information on the basis of what is already known. It uses mental short cuts when information is limited or to save time or energy. That's why we can make snap judgements about people, for example, about whether someone seems familiar, or even trustworthy. Habits and routine are natural consequences of the way our brains are configured. We can do something over and over again until, eventually, we don't even have to think about it.

Our habitual natural tendencies can be incredibly helpful and sensible (putting a seat belt on without thinking, washing our hands after the loo, stopping at a red light). Habits help us to size up the world, warn us of danger and make decisions without effort. But some of them can imprison us. They can lead to us unthinkingly processing any new incoming information according to what we know, rather than on the basis of what we are actually perceiving. Or they can lead us to do things mindlessly, without stopping to think about what we are doing. Not surprisingly, sometimes the brain is pulled up short when it has to face patterns, people and behaviours that are different to what we know or habitually do. Processing them requires conscious effort and a forging of new pathways outside the 'comfort zone' of the familiar. But when we make ourselves do so we are freed up from the old automatic habits and no longer locked into the old ways. That's why, if you can change what you do, you can change your future.

> There's nothing better for the brain than to bombard
> it with things it has never encountered before. New
> sights, new sounds, new smells, new actions and
> new perceptions. Because it's only when the brain
> is confronted with things it has never come across
> before that it begins to reorganize itself. Potentially,
> to lay down new pathways. Ones that supplant the
> old ones.

The neuroscientist Gregory Berns describes novelty as
a trigger for running the automatic system in reverse,

> *so that an individual can see things that she didn't
> see before simply by employing her attention
> differently. But it is impossible to do this under
> 'business-as-usual' conditions. It typically takes a
> novel stimulus – either a new piece of information or
> getting out of the environment in which the individual
> has been comfortable...*

The programme in this book has tried to steer you off
the regular track and render you more receptive to
change. It's been doing this by getting you to question
your habits and natural tendencies. By forcing you to
act more consciously and be more mindful of how you
behave. That's the way in which you'll set yourself free
of your old dependency on smoking. We know that if
left to its own devices the brain would have you behave
in the ways you have always done. It slips into addiction too readily. But sometimes we have to distract it
from its usual ways. That's why interrupting the brain's
automatic responses is the key to knocking the smoking habit on the head for good. And you never know,

you might spot new solutions to problems that haven't appeared on your mental radar before.

We hope this method has convinced you that, when it comes to breaking out of old ways, trying to *think* differently will be a poor lever for change. *Doing* something different is powerful because only when a natural tendency is displaced by a new *action* is change possible.

Sometimes it's good for us to do what doesn't come naturally. How many exciting, daring or unusual adventures have you had in the past year? How many will you have in the year to come? In the words of Greg Berns again, 'The solution is to seek out environments in which you have no experience.' When did *you* last do that?

By following the Do Something Different programme every day, you will not only seek out new experiences but you'll also expand your behavioural flexibility. This helps you get the most out of all situations and relationships. Some of the DSD techniques nudge you into seeing things differently, to raise your awareness. This makes you more open to fresh opportunities that were hidden behind your old, one-dimensional approach, perhaps opening doors that you'd never even noticed before.

What's more, by doing what comes *un*naturally, you'll be more likely to notice the consequences of the non-routine behaviours. You'll spot that when you do something different, you get something different. You'll be acting on the world instead of letting it act upon you. That means more self-responsibility, which is vital for effectiveness in all areas of your life. And more open-mindedness, which can mean better relationships and far less stress. Never underestimate the power that changing yourself has on other people: bosses, colleagues, friends, partners and lovers, in positive ways.

It's all about expanding your world, one small behaviour at a time. Seeking out unfamiliar situations and environments with which you have no experience. These novel environments will contain none of the old triggers that caused you to smoke, and are fertile ground in which to forge new ways of behaving.

Fear of the Unknown

By now we hope you have learned not to be too fearful of the unknown. You've already coped with doing new things in old situations. And we hope you've felt the buzz that comes from doing something different. If you still get a flicker of foreboding when confronted with the prospect of venturing outside your comfort zone, that's a natural reaction.

Your habit machine of a brain loves nothing more than being able to predict what's going to happen next. If it can't, it sends you that familiar twinge of apprehension via the *amygdala*, an almond-shaped structure located deep in the brain. The amygdala is like a cranky old bear with a long memory, who can't forget all the unpleasant things that have happened in the past. He's exceptionally wary of anything slightly unfamiliar. The way to keep him in check is to know that the fear response is trying to paralyze you, to stop you facing the unknown, and then to go ahead and face it. Susan Jeffers hit the nail on the head with her book title *Feel the Fear and Do It Anyway*. Paradoxically, although fear is an inhibitor of action, action is an excellent antidote to fear.

You can also use some devious thinking strategies to overcome fear of the unknown. A popular one is called *cognitive reappraisal*, which simply involves changing what you tell yourself about an impending event. By doing this you suppress the amygdala and recruit the brain's more sensible prefrontal cortex, to regain control over the fear. Michael Heppell's book *Flip It* is full of ideas for turning things on their heads and looking at them in a different way. He points out that when you reinterpret situations in novel ways, they seem far less frightening. Here are some examples:

- Instead of worrying about feeling like an amateur when joining a new group, you tell yourself it's an opportunity to learn.
- Instead of fearing criticism for behaving in a different way, you reframe it as a chance to get feedback. Then you choose whether it's helpful or not.
- Even losing your job might be reinterpreted as being granted freedom and seen as a wake-up call to pursue a dream.
- Allen Carr's advice of saying you are going to 'stop' smoking rather than 'give up' smoking might help you to see the quitting process as less of a sacrifice and more of a decision.

A lot of fear is fear of failure. Yet successful people don't fail any less than the rest of us. They simply learn from failure and reframe it as a good place from which to start again. Henry Ford, the motor manufacturer, in his book *My Life and Work*, gives a good example of how to reframe failure: 'Failure is only the opportunity more intelligently to begin again. There is no disgrace in honest failure; there is disgrace in fearing to fail.'

We have a friend who hated going to mundane meetings for his council job. But he reframed them as 'being paid to daydream' and is now building a boat and planning his next exciting life goal.

In this programme we encourage you to reframe your view of quitting smoking. Not to see it as giving something up but as *getting something back*. Getting back your health, your money, your relationships and your life. But we add a note of caution, too. Getting the right mindset is only a small part of the solution. Thinking differently alone won't make you into a non-smoker. You also need to Do Something Different.

Q&A

Next you're going to think about some of the habits you have in relation to the relationships you have with the people you interact with and the things you do in your everyday life. Try to answer the following questions honestly by considering what you think is your natural tendency.

First, relationships: to how many of these would you say 'Yes'?

Do you like to do things that others are doing? ☐

Do you tend to take people's casual remarks quite personally? ☑

At a party do you let others make the first move? ☑

Do you socialize with the same people most of the time? ☑

Are most of your friends from the same race/class as you? ☐

Are you able to judge people quickly? ☐

Do you hold grudges against people? ☐

Are you quick to see other people's faults? ☐

Do you find it hard to give compliments to others or praise them? ☐

Do you see the differences in others as their problem? ☐

Are you bothered about the reactions of other people? ☐

When things go wrong, is it usually due to other people? ☐

Are there types of people with whom you just can't get along? ☐

Do you avoid taking issues up with people? ☑

Do you think some people are just not worth talking to? ☐

Are some people just lucky to be where they are? ☐

Do you wait for others to contact you? ☑

Do you think that other people should contact you when it is their turn? ☐

Do you have people in your life with whom you have fallen out? ☐

Do you avoid people who are not important to you? ☐

Do you have few friends? ☐

Do you sometimes give other people's confidences/ secrets away? ☐

Do you feel jealous at the good fortune of your friends? ☐

Do you relish the opportunity to gossip about people? ☐

Do you think others should make an effort to understand you? ☐

Do you think it is unnecessary to be polite to other people? ☐

TOTAL ___

How Did You Do?

To how many of the above questions did you answer 'Yes'? Check the box that corresponds to your total score.

☑ Fewer Than 5 (LOW)

Great! You don't appear to be particularly habitual in your interactions with people. This should help you to avoid getting into habitual ways of interacting and, if you do, to recognize what these are and do something about it. Your score suggests you can see the value in many different types of people, not just those who are like you. You are also flexible in your approach to people and your open-mindedness means you have the potential for an active and varied social life. Make the most of this now and relish every opportunity to mix with different people in new social situations. Enjoy trying some of the Relationship DSDs in the coming week to really make the most of your interpersonal skills.

☐ Between 5 and 10 (MEDIUM)

Like many people you show a tendency to have a range of habits that are related to how you view others and behave toward them. Your score suggests you have a tendency to stick to the people you know and aren't always welcoming of differences. But people who don't think like you may have a lot to offer in terms of different perspectives and new insights. If you open yourself up to them you could get a richer experience. You could be missing out on good relationships simply because you rule some people out of your social circle. Or perhaps you've got out of the habit of putting the effort into relationships? The more you can change these habits, the more you will be able to reinvent yourself as a life-long non-smoker. To be stimulated by adventure, new environments, meeting strangers and moving around. Take advantage of some of the Relationship DSDs in the coming week to ensure you're really making the most of all the interactions in which you engage.

☐ More Than 10 (HIGH)

You appear to recognize that you have some fixed ideas when it comes to relationships. The interactions you have may be compromised because you tend to make snap judgements about people rather than giving them the benefit of the doubt or seeing how things unfold. Perhaps you've recognized your tendency to gravitate toward certain types of people, those who are like you and with whom you feel comfortable rather than those from a different background? This is a sound basis from which to develop because you can already see the areas in which you need to make changes. Although trying new ways of interacting and mixing with different people may feel a bit uncomfortable at first, it's worth dipping a toe into the discomfort zone and trying some new ways of interacting. When you gradually learn to get the best out of all the relationships you have, you'll

feel more at ease with yourself and less likely to succumb to social anxieties or stress. The coming week
has plenty of opportunities to make this come about
and to bring new perspectives to your relationships.

To how many of these would you say 'Yes'?

Do you often say you are going to do something and fail to do it?	☑
Do you have a backlog of things you should have done?	☑
Do you say one thing and do another?	☐
When someone wants to share a problem, do you try to fix it?	☑
Do you stick to what you know when faced with a choice?	☐
Do you lack the time to do the things you would like to do?	☐
Do you think it's hard to fit things you want to do into your daily routine?	☐
Do you think that it is too late in life to be how you would have liked to be?	☐
Do you worry what other people will think if you do things the way you want to?	☐
Are you bothered about the reactions of other people?	☐
Are there times when you fail to do what you think is right?	☑
Do you think it is impossible to get enjoyment from ordinary daily activities (such as gardening and housework)?	☐
Do you tend to do things in the same way?	☐

Are you the kind of person who stays in the background and prefers not to be noticed? ☐

Do you overeat or drink too much alcohol? ☐

Do you try to get others to do things for you? ☐

Do you think you were born the way you are and that it is difficult to do things very differently? ☐

Do you think of yourself as having a strong personality? ☐

Do you have set times for when you eat? ☑

Does the day often fly by? ☐

Do you think it is difficult for a person to change? ☐

Do you often go on holiday to the same place? ☐

Do you have regular nights for doing things? ☐

Do you get bothered if people move your things from where they should be? ☐

TOTAL ___

How Did You Do?

To how many of the above questions did you answer 'Yes'? Check the box that corresponds to your total score.

☑ Fewer Than 5 (LOW)

Excellent. You're definitely more of a Dora the Explorer than a stick-in-the-mud. You're not too set in your ways when it comes to your 'Activity' habits. This means you are open to trying new things and are not too wedded to your old ways and routines. Novelty comes fairly easy to you so you should find it relatively easy to increase the range of things that you do and to seek out unfamiliar experiences and fresh environments. Make sure that when you choose your Activity DSDs in the next section you find some that really do stretch you and push your limits a little further.

☐ Between 5 and 10 (MEDIUM)

OK, you show a tendency to have some habits that might mean you're not leading as full a life as you could. Or that you've closed too many doors in the past, perhaps due to fear or a reluctance to explore new territory. Let's hope this programme has already started to open your eyes to new ways of doing things. When you choose some Activity DSDs from the list on the next pages, do try to overcome your natural reluctance and be a bit more adventurous than you've been lately. Squash your fear of the unknown and the coming week will be another time of growth for you.

☐ More Than 10 (HIGH)

You appear to recognize that you have many thinking habits related to the things you do. This is a sound basis from which to develop because at least you can see the areas in which you might benefit from injecting a few changes. But first of all you might like to reassure yourself that the world won't fall apart if you don't do things the way you've always done them. Perhaps staying stuck in the mud might explain why you stayed a smoker for so long? No doubt you'll have heard the expression many times that life isn't a rehearsal. Nor is it a dance that should be sat out, so jump up and join in. By hanging on to old ways you deny the possibility of the mysterious unknown; the possibility that life can be much better.

What to Do Next

Look up your scores (Low/Medium/High) for the Relationships and Activity questions on pages 208 and 211 to see where you are in the table. This will guide you toward some Do Something Different tasks – DSDs – for the next seven days. The table below will show you how to plan your tasks for the next week. According to your score on each of the questionnaires you've just filled in (Relationships and Activity), the table will indicate how many tasks, and of which type, to do in the coming week. It's a very expansive list so you can choose the ones most appropriate to you – and do lots more than those allotted if you wish to.

For example, if you scored High on the Relationships questionnaire and Low on the Activity questionnaire, this week you will do one Activity DSD on one day and six Relationships DSDs on the other days. Or, if you scored Low on the Relationships questions and Low on the Activity questions, this week you would do Activity DSDs on four days and Relationships DSDs on three days.

	Low Activity Score	Medium Activity Score	High Activity Score
Low Relationships Score	3 Activity & 4 Relationships DSDs	5 Activity & 2 Relationships DSDs	6 Activity & 1 Relationships DSDs
Medium Relationships Score	2 Activity & 5 Relationships DSDs	3 Activity & 4 Relationships DSDs	5 Activity & 2 Relationships DSDs
High Relationships Score	1 Activity & 6 Relationships DSDs	2 Activity & 5 Relationships DSDs	3 Activity & 4 Relationships DSDs

You'll find the Relationships and Activity DSDs on pages 216–21. It doesn't matter on which days you do them, so long as you do at least as many of each type of task over the next seven days as the table indicates. Yours will add up to seven, so that means at least one a day, but do more if you can.

You'll be choosing the tasks from a list of 50 – and there are some key points to bear in mind when you choose your DSDs:

1. Don't choose something you do normally; be different and daring.
2. Choose something just outside your comfort zone; something that makes you feel just a bit uncomfortable. If it feels easy to do, it probably isn't working.
3. Remember, a DSD gives you licence to behave a bit differently or try something new (but always behave appropriately).

The DSD programme in the coming week offers you the chance to expand and grow – and who knows where that might take you? Nick Baylis writes about people's wonderful lives (in his book uncannily named *Wonderful Lives*). He recounts how individuals' small changes were often instrumental in bringing about big gains in their lives. He says: 'Bearing in mind that our knowledge-based society pays quite a premium for original perspectives, this strategy of "doing something different" could prove highly profitable on any number of fronts.' Make Do Something Different your mantra.

Relationships DSDs: Changing How You Are with People

Depending on your score, you are now going to choose a number, from one to six, of Relationships DSDs from the list on the next page. Remember, don't cheat and pick an easy option. If you do you'll simply perpetuate the present, and this is all about shaping the future. For example, 'Make tea for other people' would not be at all challenging if you work in a café. But let's say you're a company director or boss who's stereotypically managerial. How about if one day you offered to make tea for your staff? That might ruffle your image and push you out of your comfort zone, true enough. But it might also help your staff and colleagues to see you in a different light (he's actually just like us!). It could help you to appreciate what others who work for you do and, in the end, who knows, might even improve relationships.

Similarly, the 'join a group' DSD might not be a big ask for someone who's naturally gregarious and in every club in town. That's not a DSD for them. But for the shyer, more withdrawn type this could provide the impetus to make that push and open up a new social world. Oh, and if you're already married/attached, can we politely suggest you give the 'Find a partner' DSD a miss? (Although don't rule out the 'Go on a date with my partner' DSD if you haven't done that in a while.)

The trick this week is to try to be open to new people or new ways of being in old relationships. Remember, if you always hang around with people you agree with, and only ever read things that confirm what you already know, or only ever listen to views that match your own, you're never challenging your existing brain connections. Seek out diversity, variety and novel experiences with as many different people as you can.

When you look at the DSDs in the two lists, choose the ones that are really *different* for you. Remember, the discomfort zone is where progress occurs, and unless you Do Something Different, the present will become permanent.

Get your free Habit-Breaker Cards at www.lovenotsmoking.com. Use these cards whenever the old urges threaten to creep up on you. Remember, it's important to stay active to keep up your resolve.

Relationships DSDs

Choose from This List – and Stretch Yourself

Make the first move to repair a broken friendship	
Stop interrupting people and listen more	
Come up with three good conversation-starter questions	✓
Share laughter with at least three people	
Stop blaming others and take responsibility	
Help my kids to follow their passions	
Tell a joke to a stranger	
Stop hanging on to the past and move on	
Act confident when nervous	
Spend time with someone much older	

Ask advice from someone much younger	
Examine one of my strongly held beliefs and question it	
✗ Tell friends why I like them	✓
Smile more, moan less	
Admit that a bad relationship isn't working	
Open up to someone/confess	
Act as if I already am the person I want to be	
Plan a surprise for a friend	
Give more compliments	
See things from the other person's perspective	
Take a risk with someone	✓
Choose a different name for myself	
Send some money to someone anonymously	
Have more meaningful conversations	✓
Plan to spend time with positive people	✓
Admit when I am wrong	
Go and visit someone who can't get out	✓
Give more hugs	✓
Let my family teach me new things about myself	
✗ Pay more attention to personal grooming	✓
Phone instead of texting/emailing	
Be more polite to people	
Find a partner	✓
Express my gratitude to someone I've taken for granted	✓
Invite neighbours round for a drink or a coffee	✓

Show genuine interest in other people	✓
Be the first to say 'Hi'	
Bake a cake for a neighbour	
Leave a 'Thank You' card for someone I don't know	✓
Join that group I've heard about	
Organize a social event for friends/colleagues	
⚹ Look around for another job	✓
Go on a date with my partner	
Make tea for other people	
Learn a few words of my neighbours' language	
Rock the boat if necessary	
Set my sights higher	✓
Stop wishing and start doing	✓
Connect three of my friends with each other	
Meet a friend for breakfast	

Activity DSDs: Changing an Activity Habit

Choose from one to six of the tasks from the list below depending on how you scored on the table on page 214. Remember, your heart and lungs will be recovering their function without the crippling effects of smoking, so make the most of your newfound energy!

Buy a magazine I wouldn't normally get, and read it	
Change radio stations, or start listening to one	✓
Let another person choose from the menu for me	
Get on a bus and see where it takes me	✓

Wear shorts to the office	
Go to a public meeting or local town hall	✓
Hang out at a live sporting event	
Do a painting, collage or drawing	✓
Find a local charity group and go and help out	✓
Do that DIY job I've been putting off	
Go to the cinema by myself	
Contact a long-lost friend or relation	✓
Visit an art gallery	✓
Write an impressive CV for myself	
Go skating or roller-blading	✓
Learn to meditate	
Read a different newspaper	
Drive in a less aggressive manner	
Dance under the stars	✓
Make more lists	✓
Pay off a debt	
Sign up for a dance class	
Cycle to work	
Play louder music	
Apply for that dream job	✓
Get a temporary tattoo and wear it somewhere visible	
Wear a ring on a thumb or toe	
Go disco dancing or learn to tango/salsa/tap dance	
Repair or renew something that's broken	✓
Listen to a new kind of music	
Let my hair down and do something out of character	✓

De-junk an area of my home; get rid of clutter	✓
Clear up after myself	
Go barefoot	✓
Give up something that's damaging me	✓
✗ Restyle my image or get advice on how to	✓
Go skinny-dipping	
Put a time limit on stuff I spend too long on	✓
Turn up at the cinema and watch the next film that's starting	
Open a book at random and read for half an hour	✓
Be mindful on a walk or journey; take notes or photos	✓
Plan to go to an unusual holiday destination	
Find out about volunteering	✓
Leave my watch off for a day	
✗ Go without my mobile for a day	✓
Get a new hairstyle	✓
Throw out some old photographs	✓
Resist the pull of a temptation	✓
Spend more time in a different environment (city/country)	✓
Stop saying I'm going to do something and do it	✓

Now you should have at least seven DSDs in total from the two lists.

Have another look at them and ask yourself:

1. On a scale of one to ten, how much does this push me out of my comfort zone (where one is not at all and ten is extreme discomfort)? Try to choose something that is at least a six and mildly uncomfortable.
2. On a scale of one to ten, how different is the DSD from what I would normally do (where one is not at all and ten is extremely different)? Try to choose something that is at least a six and quite different.

Then, when you have selected the right sort of DSDs for you, go ahead to the next stage. This is the phase where you plan your own tailored DSD programme to follow in the coming week. Write one of your chosen DSDs (from the preceding lists) into the daily planner that follows, one for each day, until you have filled up the seven days.

Also keep the Habit-Breaker Cards with you (www.lovenotsmoking.com). Use them as you did last week, to interrupt an automatic response or disrupt a craving if you find you need to. And don't forget that pledge you wrote on Day 11 containing all the reasons why you are quitting. Keep it handy as a reminder and so you don't lose sight of those all-important reasons.

WEEKLY PLANNER
MY RELATIONSHIPS AND ACTIVITY DSDs
for week ending ....

Day 29 Date: ...~~February~~ 22nd/22

Which DSD are you doing today?

ACTIVITY ☐ **RELATIONSHIPS** ☑

Note down here what you are going to do (from the lists):

Come up with 3 good conversation-starter questions .

....

Day 30 Date: ~~February~~ 24

Which DSD are you doing today?

ACTIVITY ☐ **RELATIONSHIPS** ☑

Note down here what you are going to do (from the lists):

Tell friends why I like them *

....

....

Day 31   Date: Feb 28th

Which DSD are you doing today?

ACTIVITY ☑   **RELATIONSHIPS** ☐

Note down here what you are going to do (from the lists):

Dance under the stars!

♡

Day 32   Date: March 2nd

Which DSD are you doing today?

ACTIVITY ☑   **RELATIONSHIPS** ☐

Note down here what you are going to do (from the lists):

Restyle my image or get advice how to.

Day 33   Date: March 10th

Which DSD are you doing today?

ACTIVITY ☑   **RELATIONSHIPS** ☐

Note down here what you are going to do (from the lists):

.....Go without my mobile for a day.

.....Also maybe the art gallery......

....

Day 34   Date: ....

Which DSD are you doing today?

ACTIVITY ☐   **RELATIONSHIPS** ☐

Note down here what you are going to do (from the lists):

....

....

....

Day 35   Date: ~~Feb~~ March 1st

Which DSD are you doing today?

ACTIVITY ☑   RELATIONSHIPS ☐

Note down here what you are going to do (from the lists):

Go to art museum.

Get your free Habit-Breaker Cards at www.lovenotsmoking.com. Use these cards if you still feel you need to; they'll stop you slipping back onto auto-pilot.

Love Not Smoking Fact: Don't lose sight of the power of exercise in helping you through the quit period and beyond. Hopefully by now exercise has become more of a daily habit, or you've upped your activity levels. Researchers from the University of Exeter have found that short bouts of exercise make a huge difference in helping quitters stay smoke-free. Physical activity, such as a brisk walk, helped the participants in their study with weight maintenance as well as managing the withdrawal symptoms.

People who did exercise were also less affected by seeing someone else light up; they weren't as tempted by this as were the more sedentary folk. Choose exercise that you enjoy and you're more likely to stick with it.

Week 6

FULL BEHAVIOUR OPTIMIZATION

Welcome to the final week of the Love Not Smoking: Do Something Different programme. By now we guess you're beginning to feel you've left the smoking habit behind. Yes, you're a smug non-smoker and rightly proud of it. Some people tell us at this point they can't believe they ever smoked. And they tell us they love not smoking.

You've already learned from this programme how it feels to no longer be a slave to the smoking habit. You have broken free of the ugly nicotine master. In fact, you've gone beyond that because you don't need to be a slave to *any* habits now. You've probably unlearned a mind-blowingly long list of automatic behaviours as you've been through this programme. That might be enough for you now to go off and enjoy your newfound freedom and newly enriched life. You can skip to Chapter 9 from here if you're fully confident that's how you feel. Or you may wish to repeat one of the previous weeks to solidify the new you.

Or you may wish to carry on.

We should warn readers now that this week is the toughest part of the programme. But we give you an option of whether you go through it or not. It's ideal for those people who feel they've not only been on a quit-smoking programme, but have embarked on a life-changing personal journey. Some people really feel the full force of Do Something Different and reap huge transformational benefits. They get a sense of what it's like to feel in control of their lives, and they want to work at adopting this approach as a total way of living. If that's you, then please do continue with this final week. Prepare to learn more about the science behind this approach, to target some of the ways you think and behave, and to get ready for more transformation.

For the past weeks on the programme you have been *doing something different*. We now want to change direction a little and concentrate on your thinking processes. No doubt by doing something different you can't fail to have noticed that your mind has been stimulated as well. You've probably become more curious about *why* you do the things you do. The new experiences may have made you stop and reflect in all sorts of ways. After all, you have flooded your brain with new inputs: sensory and practical stimulation that it would never have had without the programme. All this will have gone on whether or not you have consciously thought about it. Unconscious inputs will have subtly altered your habit web and upset some of the automatic processes and triggers that made you smoke in the past. There will have been some cognitive consequences of this behaviour change.

We have an unshakable belief that new behaviours bring about new thinking, which is the key to all kinds of successful life changes. Our approach starts with doing something different, which then subtly inspires changes in thinking. That's a crucial outcome because, in the end, if you want to develop as a person you have got to change your mind as well as your behaviour. To cement the new behavioural habits with the right kind of thinking.

The driving power of the Do Something Different technique is how the new behaviours work on your behavioural flexibility. Each new action or novel experience expands and stretches you. This kick-starts new and constructive thinking processes. We stand by our previous arguments about the weakness of *trying* to use thinking, exhortations or negative health information to give up smoking. Those methods, based as they are upon willpower or education, fail when they are up against the massive strength of inertia and what we do habitually. But the benefits from changing thinking *can* be useful – and can happen without effort – when the old habit web has been weakened by a programme of Do Something Different.

This phase of the Love Not Smoking: Do Something Different programme brings those new thinking processes into sharper focus. It helps to bring to your attention the thought processes that are critical for doing the right things. We hope it will help foster in you a 'growth mindset'. This final phase is going to give the old automatic thoughts and habits a final push into the background and allow room for some conscious, deliberate thinking.

What are the aspects of thinking that need developing in order for you to become a better, more fulfilled person?

We've been working for many years on the answer to this important question, which comes from FIT Science. FIT stands for Framework for Internal Transformation, and it was founded by Ben more than 20 years ago. The Do Something Different techniques grew independently out of FIT Science. FIT Science accurately defines and represents the profile of a person with below average stress and a successful and well-balanced life. FIT people have more satisfying jobs and relationships; they have greater physical and mental wellbeing and they are able to cope with whatever life throws at them.

FIT Science itself does not provide the techniques to bring about change. Do Something Different fits that bill. But FIT outlines the five key aspects of thinking that underpin a solid psychological base for life. We call these 'Inner FIT Constancies', and they are:

1. Awareness
2. Fearlessness
3. Self-responsibility
4. Balance
5. Conscience

It is these pillars of Inner FIT thinking that you are going to become more familiar with in this final phase, as Ben talks you through each of them. Working through these constancies will build up your inner resources, equipping you to do the right thing in future. That includes all aspects of having a more fulfilled life – as well as not backsliding into taking up smoking again, of course – and giving you a firm psychological base from which to move forward.

Awareness

This is the degree to which you monitor and attend to your internal and external worlds. It is how awake and conscious you are of all relevant aspects of yourself and the situation you are in.

Awareness is the engine and monitor of being FIT. When you think about it, it is the opposite of habits and natural tendencies, since we know these tend to spring forth without us noticing. Raising your sense of awareness is about attending to the thoughts you are having, and the sensory information you are experiencing, in the moment.

A central aspect of awareness involves paying attention to 'relevant' detail and from all perspectives. We all become habituated to looking at the world through old eyes. Due to the way the brain is configured, and our propensity for habits, we see and sense what we have seen and sensed before. But there is so much more available for our senses to see than what our automatic pilot points us toward. Consider all the sensory information from the environment around you. Determine how you are sitting, precisely what made you read this, how aware you have been over the last 30 seconds, what sights and sounds have been going on around you. How aware were you of all the factors at work in the last interaction you had with someone: the words they were using, the subtle expressions on their face or their body language? Sometimes we are so wrapped up in what we are doing or saying that we tune out what's going on around us. The more aware we are, the less chance that our choices will be constrained by seeing only part of the picture.

But awareness includes more that just 'attention' to the things going on in the environment. It also includes awareness of your own motives and needs, and awareness of the likely motives and needs of others. It includes self-awareness in the broadest sense, one that involves getting to know your feelings and thoughts, and how these steer your own actions. This can take some time and practice – depending on how deeply you've allowed your habits to bury your awareness. But with awareness comes an opening up of options, too, and a knowledge of when there are more choices available than we thought. So the awareness constancy is also the options and possibilities guide, and makes for a more expansive world.

Today: Awareness

Focus on this constancy today and see how it can drive your thinking and behaviour.

Increase your awareness to be alert to all kinds of previously unnoticed aspects inside and around you. Broaden your channels of attention to take in things you go past every day without noticing. Listen to sounds in your environment: birdsong, the wind in the leaves. Look up instead of down and notice the roofs, the clouds, the stars. Ask someone to give you feedback about something you've done/said. Stay a little longer with a friend or colleague and give them your full attention. Try to feel the emotions they are feeling, digest their words as if they were your own. Focus intensely on something you do automatically (like eating, washing or resting), savour every detail and experience all the sensations mindfully. Be present.

Fearlessness

This is acting without fear or trepidation, or essentially facing the unknown with the same bravado as the known.

Doing things without fear is important, not only for our emotional wellbeing but also to help us make the right decisions and act upon them. If we are fearful about future situations, we are going to be reluctant to venture forth. Habit makes us retreat back into the safe, the known and the comfortable. Yet we know that fear is a major force that can intrude on the decision-making processes and behaviours of many people. It affects us all at times. In my view, fear has no purpose whatever in shaping decisions and behaviour in the modern world, although I am aware that many people disagree with this. When giving talks on FIT Science over the years, I (Ben) have been challenged to support my view. I do see that fear may have some primal functions and would have protected primitive humans from predators, but that is in the past, or in a completely different context. We, in the West, do not roam the open plains anymore, and the parallels between ancient demands and modern society are, in my view, losing their relevance. One has to question seriously nowadays the purpose – for a cognitive human being – of fear in any situation. Sure, if I am on the edge of a big drop I will be fearful, but I don't think that fear is protective there, either – speaking for myself only, I wonder if the sensation of fear might even make me more likely to fall! It might even make some jump.

Being fearless is not just about doing things without the feeling of fear surfacing in your thoughts. In some situations it is actually better to acknowledge the fear but still to do the right thing. A person who can behave fearlessly is able to make the right choices without being swayed by the feelings of fear that threaten to engulf them. So a 'fearless' decision, of course, may bring with it a temporary feeling of fearfulness. In this context I am reminded of one person whose FIT Profiler (an instrument we use to measure people on each of the constancies) clearly showed him to be low on the fearless constancy. Over time he was profiled several times and always objected to being categorized as fearful, insisting that fear did not drive his decisions and hardly featured in his life. The penny dropped one day when he realized he had designed his life to make sure he never encountered the situations or things that might cause him to feel fearful. He had made his life a safe haven, kept the unknown at bay, and so had almost guaranteed that he would never encounter fear in his life. As a result, however, his world had shrunk. He wasn't making the most of life's possibilities and felt he was missing out on opportunities – and that was one reason he was really being held back.

Here we come to another important point about fearlessness. To be fully alive and expand our world, it is necessary to unearth the fears beneath the natural tendencies we all have. These hidden fears, if left unchallenged and lurking, can do us far more damage than if we confront the fears and overcome them. The family of fear drives many behaviours and decisions that people make, although these are often not apparent. Fear can have a strong grip on our unconscious actions and often does not allow our conscious thoughts in on this secret. So we need to be fully aware of the hidden traps.

How many people shrink from doing something out of the ordinary, wearing different clothes or telling the boss he's wrong, or staying late just because others do? How many people do you know who have cocooned themselves in ways that allow little of the unknown into their lives? How many of their narratives include talk about doing something 'risky' (or risqué), even though they never actually take the steps needed? Fear has a tight grip on most people most of the time. And gradually they have grown accustomed to the constraints it places upon them. They may even be comforted by the presence of the negative feeling itself. For many the grip is not one over their conscious processes, but they have become so tightly bound that even their unconscious decisions and behaviours are reined in.

What can you do if you suspect you are fearful or your life is constrained due to your reluctance to face the unknown or go against the grain? Fearlessness is something that develops with experience. It is possible to achieve greater fearlessness when you do what is right for the right reasons and, by so doing, discover that the benefits far outweigh the temporary discomfort. The 'discomfort zone' can become part of your 'comfort zone' in the longer term if you learn to live without fear. The feeling of entering this unknown is not the same as the negative aspects of fear, which generally become the principal shapers of people's lives.

Today: Fearlessness

Focus on this constancy today and become alert to how it can drive your thinking and behaviour. Make decisions based on what is the right thing, rather than on what feels most comfortable. Make sure you do not choose the 'easy' option out of fear. Try to work gradually on reducing your level of fear. Push yourself to encounter at least one fearful condition (speaking out, asking a difficult question, tackling a taboo subject, going into a situation you've been avoiding). Was the fear greater than the reality? Did the benefits justify taking action? Where will you venture next?

Self-responsibility

This is the degree to which an individual accepts personal accountability for their world, irrespective of the impact of factors outside themselves.

People get what they take responsibility for. That is true of you and me. It is true for all of us. If ten different people are put in the same situation, what each makes of it will be more determined by their levels of self-responsibility than by their talents or skills. I am not sure most people believe this. It seems to me – when I listen to others talk in most situations – that people have a view that the world 'out there' determines what happens to them. Many of their opinions are prefaced with the word 'they'. 'They' are those faceless others who seem so central to the lives of people – 'they' seem to be perceived to be the primary shapers. There are many 'theys' for all of us, but it seems to be another truth that we get what we get because we think and act *as if* 'they' control things, not *because* they do.

In essence, most people mistakenly believe they do not have the power to change their lives. There are all sorts of reasons people feel they cannot take self-responsibility (nature, nurture, genes, dependents, the government), but to maximize the opportunity in any situation – however constrained it is – it is essential to be self-responsible and not limit the alternatives yourself. Let the situation do all the limiting that will happen.

In essence, the self-responsibility constancy is about removing the psychological constraints we all put on our options and actions. It's about not letting others 'take the rap' or making excuses for the way we are or the things that happen to us. It is about living as if we are god in our own universe. Its essence is in the saying, 'The world is a reflection of yourself.' What opportunities are missed because people like the comfort zone of dependence and passivity? Because people are reluctant to exercise the freedom and control they have?

Don't Wait for Catastrophe to Force Change

Although it's sad and regrettable when people suffer a major life event or catastrophe – perhaps a major illness, a partner leaving, an accident, the unexpected death of someone dear – these events do sometimes release people from the vice-like grip of their habitual ways of behaving. All sorts of changes happen as a result, and many a catastrophe ends up with some glimmer of a silver lining. In the aftermath of a catastrophic event the affected person is somehow given licence to do things they had previously wanted to do – perhaps give up a job, travel somewhere, lose weight, shake off an addiction, make a big change in daily life. It is a pity – and unnecessary – if this can only happen because of some seismic shift in circumstance or, worse still, a disaster or traumatic event. Surely it's preferable for you to make the move to improve things now, by putting yourself in the driver's seat?

A Word about Luck

The word 'luck' crops up regularly in conversations about people's attributions of success and failure. Along with fate, destiny and even horoscopes, it seems knitted into the fabric of many people's lives. I think luck will fill the vacuum if self-responsibility is not exercised. So, the degree to which you believe in luck may be a strong (inverse) barometer of your own level of self-responsibility. Our lives may be shaped by external forces, but only an absence of inner direction and choice will allow 'luck', good or bad, the chance to reign. Research makes it clear that being lucky is not a random happenstance – we make our own luck by our behaviours, by our efforts and by our own attributions. Chance, it is often said, favours the prepared mind. Random factors, synchronicity, astrological charts and supernatural forces only operate in a world where choices are not shaped and taken. The only way to predict the future is to design it.

Life's Narrative for Oneself

Doubtless we all agree that the world is 'out there' and objective in some important sense. Yet each of our objective worlds is very different. We see things in different ways. No two people's views of an event are the same. Personal perspectives feel as real to the perceiver as does the objective world itself. True self-responsibility comes from first determining and then shaping the narrative by which we live our own life. If we hide behind a story that gods, destiny or even demons have shaped us, or that luck and fate will intervene, then it will be so. I have tried to live my life being in charge of what happens, even though sometimes I have been at best a poor conductor, and other times an apparent victim of circumstance. Yes, events have sometimes seemed to conspire against me, but I have still lived with the conviction that *I* was responsible for what occurred. If it is a false belief, I cannot see that it is a harmful one. In fact, I have not been a victim of circumstance, however it seemed at the time – I have been a victim only of myself and my level of self-responsibility.

So the most important person to convince is yourself.

Today: Self-responsibility

Focus on this constancy today and see how it can drive your thinking and behaviour.

Imagine, for a moment, that you are responsible for everything in your life. That no one else has the power to make you happy or sad, weak or strong. What would you do differently? What action would you take that you've been leaving to others or leaving to chance? How would being responsible affect the choices and decisions you make? Don't make excuses or blame others. Stop saying you'll 'see what happens'. Take full responsibility for creating the life you want. Let go of the need to attribute outcomes and circumstances to external factors such as fate, luck, the tarot, tea leaves or your horoscope. If you made your own destiny, what would it look like? Be sure you are shaping life, not allowing yourself to be shaped.

Balance

Balance involves making sure each and every area of your life receives due care and attention. For any aspect of life, balance is derived from an equivalence between the level of importance, the level of effort put into it and the satisfaction resulting from it.

The balance constancy is the one that judges both value and worth. It isn't simply about the balance of time spent between work and leisure. A balanced life in the FIT sense is more than that: it's when there are integration and symmetry between the various dimensions of your life. True balance comes from acting to ensure that the appropriate level of focus is applied to each. Many people I have met have lives that are out of balance because they are too embroiled in one area of their life to the detriment of the others. Many have a real imbalance between what they say and do in different areas, too.

Balance has two different aspects:

1. The balance between **importance, satisfaction and effort**. I call this **levels balance**.
2. The balance between **different areas of life**. I call this **life balance**.

Levels Balance
Levels balance is achieved when the importance level, satisfaction level and effort level are equivalent. The levels in each measure might be high or low, but they need to be the same. Imbalance or low balance occurs, for example, if you think something is important (e.g. a particular relationship, an activity you do, or a value you hold) but do not derive the requisite amount of satisfaction from it, or do not put in the appropriate level of effort to maintain it at that level. The imbalance can

be either too much or too little for each of these three factors.

Life Balance

In terms of life balance, past research in FIT Science has concentrated on three particular elements of life:

1. Work (labour)
2. Non-work or domestic, social and personal (people)
3. Self

The key here is to create a life that has balance between all three areas.

A great deal of attention in the media and academic research has been placed on work–life balance. Many people, especially in demanding jobs where they have autonomy over when and how they work, fail to balance work and home life. This can have quite marked effects on health and wellbeing, and obviously affects personal relationships, bonding and longer-term social aspects with family and children.

This focus on work–life balance also fails to account for the importance of self in the equation. Sometimes when there is imbalance, or low levels of balance, we need to either change our mind or our behaviours.

A person should endeavour to achieve a harmony, balance and symmetry between these central dimensions to ensure inner balance, as well as balance between the external elements (e.g. home and work). Balance is ensuring that no one area is dominant.

A person is unFIT if, for example, they are primarily one-dimensional, or do not have balance between the various dimensions relevant to them. For example, an imbalance will occur if a person is too self-absorbed, obsessive, or if they devote too much time to a hobby, or if they are workaholic, or too focused on their children or family. That is why we encourage people, through Do Something Different, to expand their worlds. FIT people are multidimensional in the sense that they see the importance of all dimensions and strive to achieve balance within each dimension and between the different dimensions. Within each dimension there will be a need to achieve balance between the various aspects involved. In the non-work sphere, for example, this might require achieving a balance between:

- Partner
- Children
- Friends
- Leisure activities
- Wider community aspects

But, as always, with any of these there has to be consideration given to the importance, effort and satisfaction invested in and derived from each.

Today: Balance

Focus on this constancy today and see how it can drive your thinking and behaviour.

Today, review with an open mind and total honesty how important people or situations are to you. Make sure you are expending the appropriate amount of effort on things that matter to you. Then ask if you are putting great effort into something that doesn't rank as important, or brings poor satisfaction in return. This is where it may be time for a change. It may mean letting go of friendships that are one-sided or unsatisfying. Or consciously putting more effort into a relationship that means a lot to you, not just letting it drift along. In all that you do today, and all the people with whom you come in contact, evaluate the balance of importance, satisfaction and effort.

Conscience

This is determining for yourself what is right and wrong, differentiating between the two in all situations and consistently doing what is right.

The conscience constancy provides the social dimension, or the moral and ethical contexts for FIT. It determines the limits for behaviours and decisions that a person makes. Conscience should inform all decisions: personal, social and business decisions alike. In all of these one needs to take account of what is morally and ethically acceptable and what is not. One has to be aware that every decision will have an impact on others, near or far, or upon the immediate or the wider environment. The conscience dimension should not, therefore, be restricted only to certain circumstances, to those that feel 'moral'. In FIT Science, the moral and ethical choice is always the right one. There are no ifs or buts (and in this case no butts, either!). There are no compromises for personal advantage, short-term gain or hedonism, or for a good time. No matter what.

But FIT Science does not lay down moral and ethical absolutes. The guidelines within which behaviour is appropriate have to be set by you, yourself. You choose what your own values are; they are based on your experience and your judgement. FIT Science is morally relativist in this sense and allows every individual to develop their own value system.

That does not mean each individual can set arbitrary, anarchic ethical standards without due regard for society's cultural and social demands. Because what is 'right' in a given context or situation will depend on two things:

1. The other constancies: what is the right course of action from the view of being totally self-responsible, fearless, balanced and aware?
2. Universal principles: what are the appropriate moral and ethical limits of reasonable behaviour, irrespective of the situation or context?

Conscience ensures that a behaviour is both FIT and moral/ethical. This will mean:

*   Treating the thoughts, desires and actions of all people with due respect
*   Respecting the physical, intellectual and emotional space of all
*   Having an honourable and honest view of oneself and others
*   Appreciating the rights of others
*   Not being prejudiced or using stereotypes to judge others
*   At times doing something we don't want to, because it is the right thing to do

Conscience is about knowing your own values and aligning your actions, feelings and thoughts to those values. Using them as your compass. For example, if kindness and respect are what you value in your relationships, you might feel uncomfortable when people gossip or malign others. Of course, it may be hard to change a view that has become a thinking habit. As we know, these can creep up on us without us noticing. They can escape from our lips before we have time to think. But when you can override tendencies that are at odds with your values, you'll feel more at peace with yourself.

Today: Conscience

Focus on this constancy today and see how it can drive your thinking and behaviour.

Be honest and examine how often you allow yourself to be steered by values that are not part of your conscience, such as hedonism or short-termism. Are you doing something because it feels good today without regard for the long-term costs or consequences? Evaluate all your choices and actions carefully today. Don't put immediate gain first. Play the long game. Decide on your long-term values and let them shape your actions and goals. Face up to any habits you are slightly uneasy about (e.g. lies that become reality, broken promises, not living up to your values, saying one thing and doing another) and focus on being true to yourself.

Part III

RELAPSE PREVENTION

Chapter 9

STAYING SMOKE-FREE FOREVER

They say that the most voracious anti-smoking person was probably once a heavy smoker. I (Karen) was at a party just before last Christmas; there was snow on the ground and temperatures had plummeted to below zero. The party hosts had thoughtfully laid on mulled wine and a gorgeous log fire for those of us who'd ventured out. As I hugged my wine and hogged the fire, a guy next to me pointed out three people scurrying onto the patio to have a cigarette. 'Shut the door behind you,' he yelled. 'Don't let the cold in – or your fumes!' He then launched into a rant about the evil weed, about smokers being the scourge of the Earth and tobacco manufacturers nothing more than a bunch of mass murderers. How glad he was that smoking was banned in public places. 'I can't believe they used to have *smoking* sections on aeroplanes,' he said. 'That's like having a peeing section in a swimming pool.'

'Have you ever smoked?' I couldn't resist asking him. 'Oh yes,' he replied, 'I was a 40-a-day man. Gave up seven months ago tomorrow. Best thing I ever did!'

If you've found yourself ranting at parties, darting past smokers in full face mask and breathing apparatus, looking up the anti-tobacco lobby or saying, 'No thanks,

I'd rather stick hot needles in my eyes,' to anyone who even reaches for a cigarette packet, congratulations. You've joined the hallowed, sweetly scented and, dare we say, smug ranks of the ex-smokers. And we'd bet a tobacco company's gross profit margin that a herd of wild horses wouldn't drag you back into the nicotine trap. That's truly wonderful news.

But before you get too complacent, let's just stop and think for a moment about those who *will* try to tempt you back to Camp Nicotine. You know those smokers you left behind? You're a deserter. Your new cleanliness and freedom make them feel rotten. Secretly, they'd love nothing more than to see you tainted again. Then there's that sinister but irresistible anti-reasoning substance, alcohol. An excess of alcohol can sabotage the resolve of the most staunch abstainer and, let's face it, all sorts of human dilemmas have come from the inability of the inebriated to say, 'No'.

Worse still, there's the magnetic power that your old habits can still exert over you. You've been doing a fabulous job of overriding them but they may still be lurking somewhere in the dark, dusty corners of your brain. They might want to make a last-ditch attempt at survival. So it's essential that you continue to wield your clout over those habits, keep demolishing the habit web and Do Something Different at every conceivable opportunity. That said, we get amazing 'stick-ability' rates with the Love Not Smoking: Do Something Different programme, and so far our quitters are life-long quitters. Life's too good for our quitters to even consider a U-turn.

However, if the whiff of a puff of smoke still sends you into a frenzy of nostalgia and you want some extra insurance to see you through the weeks ahead, the pointers and prods on the next few pages will guarantee you stay completely smoke-free. We encourage you to avoid situations of high temptation where possible, but also know that you want life to carry on as normal, so staying alert coupled with the coping strategies you've learned will see you through.

> **Please don't kid yourself you can have 'just one cigarette'. Or even 'just one puff'. To stay free from smoking it's absolutely essential that you don't take this backwards step. Never take a puff again – no matter how long it is since you quit.**

If you do find yourself having a lapse – maybe you're out having a few drinks and someone offers you a cigarette and before you know it you've lit it and it's on your lips:

1. Stub it out straight away.
2. Tell yourself all is not lost; it was simply a slip.
3. Learn from it: how can you avoid it happening next time?
4. Don't kid yourself that you can now have the occasional cigarette, or be a 'social' smoker. Most people who think this end up being addicted again.
5. Brush up on the coping strategies you've learned so far in this book, and keep the Do Something Different message at the forefront of your mind.

The following pages will help you prevent a relapse. By this stage of the programme you're probably a DSD expert and well-versed in the art of doing something a bit out of the ordinary. We secretly hope you've got DSD in your DNA by now. In fact, we bet you could come up with tons of creative, inspiring and life-changing DSD ideas of your own. Feel free to do so … but if not, or if you want a bit of help, read on.

GIVE-IT-A-WHIRL DAY

As a non-smoker life just gets better and better, and you may start to notice all sorts of opportunities you missed before. Although habits and routines help us to manage the basics of life, they can also mask opportunities that lie just beyond the range of our immediate view. Here's a challenge: try not to say 'no' to anything today – except a cigarette, of course! Find ways of doing things you automatically think you can't do. Be open to new opportunities and accept invitations. Be a can-do, yes-person today.

What did you say yes to?

....

....

....

....

Smoke-Free Tip: Revisit the Reasons Why You Quit

Look again at the pledge you made on Day 11 of this programme. Reread it and keep it close to you.

Then remind yourself that this is probably the most positive, life-affirming thing you have ever done, and **list on the next page** all the good things that have come from quitting:

....

....

....

....

....

(The word cloud on page 265 may provide further inspiration.)

GET-DEEP DAY

As a non-smoker you'll find you're motivated to get all you can from life, and making deeper connections with people is part of that process. Try to have at least one meaningful conversation today. Forget small talk and see if you can go a little deeper and build a stronger bond with someone. To do this you may need to ask penetrating questions and be genuinely interested in the answers the other person gives. Also, be open and honest about yourself and curious about what makes those around you tick.

Reflect here:

....

....

....

Smoke-Free Tip: Keep on Moving

By getting nicotine out of your system you'll have found you have more energy. Make the most of it from now on. Whether it's a short walk, gardening, swimming, cycling or taking up rock climbing, the more exercise you can introduce into your daily routine, the greater your chances of sticking to a healthier lifestyle.

How many minutes' exercise did you get today?

....

PICK-A-BRAIN DAY

Staying habit-free means keeping busy, interested and engaged with life in all its dimensions. Get advice from someone who's an expert at something today. That person who knows about business/bee-keeping/photography/cooking – whatever; if there's anything you want to try, just ask an expert for one good tip.

Reflect here:

....

....

....

....

....

....

....

....

....

....

....

Smoke-Free Tip: Plan for Healthy Snacking

Make sure you don't have periods when you get too hungry. Snacking is fine as long as you're munching on the healthiest titbits. This might need some planning. You could keep vegetable sticks in a bag or tub in the fridge, so you're always ready for emergencies. Or stock up on dried fruits, pretzels, yoghurt and nuts. Then you won't be tempted to reach for the nearest cake when the munchies overtake!

List your favourite healthy snacks here:

....

....

....

....

....

....

....

....

NAME-DROPPERS' DAY

When we're drifting through life on autopilot, it's easy to miss stuff that's going on around us, and that can include the people we come across, too. Make the effort to learn the names of three people today. People whom you might see regularly – the postman, the person who serves you in the shop, your boss' secretary, perhaps. Write their names down if you struggle to remember names – and use them often in the future, either in conversation or just when you say, 'Hi'. There's something friendly and personal about being addressed by name.

Write their names here:

....

....

....

....

....

....

....

....

....

....

Smoke-Free Tip: Commit Those Favourite Habit-Breakers to Memory

Remember those Habit-Breaker Cards you used to distract you whenever you got a craving? Print out the three that you found most useful and make a point of memorizing them. They could be your best friends in future whenever you bump up against the triggers that used to set off an old habit. In fact, you can use your disruption technique in any situation where you're tense or wound-up – so make sure you have three of the best.

List your three disruptors here:

....

....

....

....

....

....

....

LET-IT-WASH DAY

At times some people say that they feel more irritable after quitting smoking. You may have felt this and gotten through it by now. However, some things can really get to us, if we let them. Anger, though, is never a rational response to anything, and is often destructive.

Today, instead of seething at the things that wind you up, say to yourself, 'So what?' or, 'Does it really matter?' Just let it wash over you.

Here's a selection of 'let it wash' sayings you could try:

So what?

Does it really matter?

It's not that important!

What's the worst that can happen?

Life's too short.

Why worry?

Hey ho!

Worse things happen at sea!

Who cares?

What's the big deal?

Hang loose!

Smoke-Free Tip: Brush Up on Your Relaxation Technique

Remember the relaxation technique you learned early on in the programme? Make sure you're well practised at using it. Here's how it went:

Breathe in slowly to the count of four.

Breathe out slowly to the count of four.

Just breathe as slowly and **comfortably** as you can. Counting helps you get the right pace for your relaxed breathing. After you have the timing right, say **R-E-L-A-X** slowly to yourself each time you breathe out. Do this for about five minutes.

If you haven't been using your relaxation technique regularly, why not refresh yourself, so you can use it whenever you feel tension or stress getting to you? It's a very powerful way of warding off cravings too, or simply calming the body down when things seem to be piling on top of you.

GET-AHEAD-OF-YOURSELF DAY

Get up extra early and tackle a to-do list today. Giving up smoking will have boosted your energy and given you back your sense of control – so why not use that to your advantage today? Make appointments for the future, e.g. hair, dentist, optician or chiropodist. Why not visit a dental hygienist and get your teeth thoroughly cleaned now that you're smoke-free? Put appointments in your diary so they won't get missed. Then write out cards for the next three birthdays coming up, pencilling the date to post them on the front.

Write the dates here:

....

....

....

....

....

....

....

....

Smoke-Free Tip: Plan Your Anti-Temptation Strategy

Even though you've stopped smoking, there may still be times ahead when temptation comes your way or when you feel echoes of past habits or associations. That boozy night out with your old friends, a wedding celebration or that longed-for holiday. Anticipate and prepare. Have a plan for how you'll deal with those moments. You'll know what your triggers are, or were, so work around them. You may decide to stay away from people who bother you. Or plan to avoid tricky situations. If necessary, ensure you don't get overtired and try not to be lonely. Keeping the alcohol to a minimum might be a good idea, as could avoiding the old pub. Having your Habit-Breaker Cards on you or telling friends never to offer you a cigarette would help, too.

Butt out! Write the strategy you've chosen here:

....

....

....

....

....

....

....

....

SPOT-THE-HABIT DAY

You may have kicked smoking, but general habit-busting is the secret of your sustained success. Stop and check today whether you're still being habitual. Look at the places you sit, the things you say, the places you go, the people with whom you hang out and the ways you do things – are you still predictable? Try to spot at least three habits today that you can interrupt, jiggle around or replace with something completely different

Old Habit	DSD

Smoke-Free Tip: Help Someone Else Quit

Now you know how easy it is to quit, why not pass on what you've discovered to someone else? If you know somebody who's trying to give up smoking, offer to buddy them through the process. You've been through it and come out the other end, so you have tons to offer the would-be non-smoker. Giving something back is a powerful way of maintaining a strong sense of wellbeing. And helping someone else quit will also reaffirm you as a committed non-smoker – and will ensure you stay that way for life.

Write whom you might be able to help here:

....

....

....

....

CONGRATULATIONS – YOU'VE QUIT SMOKING FOR GOOD – HOW DOES IT MAKE YOU FEEL?

Here's a word cloud made from some of the things others have said:

Chapter 10

REFLECTING ON YOUR SUCCESS

Congratulations

You now have an ashtray-free home and a smoke-free life. You are on your way to being several thousand pounds a year richer and, even as you read this, your lungs are returning to the pristine, healthy state they were in before you decided to poison them with fumes. You have become a sweeter-smelling version of your former self. You may not notice this but others, without a doubt, certainly will. Your breath will be fresher and your teeth brighter, which is a good job because you'll be smiling a lot more these days. And your fingers, without a hint of a nicotine stain, will be employed doing 101 things that make your life fulfilling and rewarding. Welcome to the new chapter of your life.

As a graduate of the Do Something Different school of non-smoking, you have been on an extraordinary and exciting personal journey of discovery. Many people tell us this programme is transformational and life-changing. We hope you agree. You have broken the stranglehold that your past habits had on you. You are no longer a slave to the nicotine master. You won't be overcompensating by eating, either, because this programme makes sure you don't use food as a cigarette substitute. You have a sense of freedom that will fast-track you to a happier and healthier life. Embrace that liberty. Remember, the key to continue getting the most from life is to keep *doing something different* and never, ever flick that life-switch back onto autopilot again. Keep using the techniques you've learned and you'll never look back.

More importantly, you have given your loved ones the greatest gift of all: the reassurance that you will never again damage your health and endanger your life by picking up a cigarette. Don't forget to thank them. Do whatever it takes to express your gratitude and your love with an open heart. If by giving you this book another person also gave you the impetus and the motivation to quit smoking, we think that's one of the most wonderful gifts any human can give to another. But the doing of it was all down to you. You are the one who followed the programme, stuck to the tasks, did as you were asked and beat off the cravings. Your loved ones will be enormously proud of you. You have signalled to them your acknowledgement of a profound commitment about what really, really matters in the world. And that's love. Not smoking.

Use this page to reflect on your experiences and discoveries, or to write a letter to yourself in the future. It could be your way of reminding yourself of the benefits of living a more flexible life, one that's free from the grip of autopilot, habit and addiction.

Chapter 11

ENOUGH ABOUT SMOKING – WHAT ABOUT LOVE?

Love. What better reason could there be to quit smoking? That's partly why we called this book *Love Not Smoking*. Another reason was that we felt you would love not smoking, and we hope that you do.

Your quitting smoking, particularly if it was for a loved one (or ones), is the best testament there is to the triumph of love over smoking. Whatever and whoever your reasons for quitting, those closest to you will be hugely proud of your achievement. Deep, loving relationships are to be treasured; they can't be bought or manufactured, and no amount of money can rescue a failing one. Sometimes, though, we get into the bad habit of letting other things take priority over our closest relationships, particularly when we are busy with the humdrum of everyday living. Even with the very best relationships, habits can creep in. When we don't pay attention to our relationship, it can stagnate. And a continued lack of investment can devalue it. Has giving up smoking made you appreciate love and life more? Awoken you to just how precious your relationships are? Why not now work on them a little to get absolutely all you can and give back as much as you can?

On the next few pages you'll find some projects to help you nurture your relationship with that special someone in your life. If a person who loves you bought you this book and you've repaid them (and yourself) by giving up smoking, what else can you do to signal to them that love, not smoking, is what really matters?

Some of the questions that people ask us include:

- How can I make my closest relationship closer?
- We've lost that sparkle – how can we get it back?
- Why doesn't my partner appreciate me like he/she used to?
- We seem to have drifted apart – what can we do about it?
- How can I invest myself fully in a relationship I've been neglecting?

The Do Something Different approach is a powerful, effective and fun way to reignite a relationship. You've seen from the exercises in this book that when *you* change it has a dynamic effect on others and often they change, too. That's why we encourage you to ask yourself, 'What am I doing to keep our love alive?' Because so often when people wonder why their relationship is less than healthy, they focus their attention heavily on what the *other person* needs to do to make it work. Or they focus on ways in which they'd like the other person to be different.

The Swiss psychiatrist and humanist Carl Jung said, 'If there is anything that we wish to change in the child, we should first examine it and see whether it is not something that could better be changed in ourselves.' This doesn't apply only to children; the principle is true for anything we might wish to change about other people.

Be the kind of person you want your loved one to be.

Here, you're not going to try to change anyone else. We all know how difficult that is, but what you're going to do is turn the spotlight on yourself. You're simply going to Do Something Different and be the kind of person you want your loved one to be. Try to portray the qualities that you value in a relationship. So if you want affection, be affectionate. If you want appreciation, be appreciative. If you want happiness, spread more happiness. Take responsibility. Change yourself first. Then see what happens...

Of course, your partner may not have the time or the inclination to join in the Do Something Different exercises that follow. They may even feel threatened by the whole idea or just think it's too wacky. Don't worry, and don't criticize them for feeling that way. Just work through one or more of the exercises yourself. If you can, talk to your partner about what you are doing and why it's something for both of you. If they've been supporting you through the Love Not Smoking: Do Something Different programme they can't have failed to notice how you've been refreshing your life and, because you love them, your partner won't be surprised that you want to make sure your relationship stays healthy. It should be vibrant and a source of pleasure and comfort for you both. But even if you do these things on your own, you'll find that your partner may gradually shift, too. That's because you will ignite new behaviours, you'll be doing something different and that will provoke a different response in others, too. It changes the temperature and the landscape of the whole relationship and paves the way for brighter and better things to come.

Listening and talking to each other are the essential ingredients of a good relationship. When communication breaks down, or people get into the habit of keeping things from their partner or losing interest in them, it's far harder to cope with tensions or troubles that arise.

That's why the exercise below gets to work on your communication skills. Don't shirk from doing things here that might make you feel a tiny bit uncomfortable at first. Embrace and enjoy trying new things and you will be repaid many times over.

Knowing Me, Knowing You

How much do you really know about your partner? How much interest do you take in their life? You may have been together a long while, but it's surprising how little even long-term partners know about each other. If you've ever seen (or played) the *Mr and Mrs* game, you'll know what we mean. Knowing – and being known – helps to build intimacy, connection and passion. That means taking the time and making the effort to question each other and disclose thoughts and feelings.

The aim of this is to find out more about your partner and their interests. That means *wanting* to find out more, too, wanting to understand the other person rather than just going through the motions. The next step is to get more involved in at least one area of their life. Engaging in this way is another means of minimizing the differences between you, creating intimacy and enriching your relationship.

What do you know about the separate parts of each other's lives?

Of course, you'll both be very familiar with the home space you share ... but what do you know about each other's workplace?

- Do you know about your partner's journey to work every day?
- Have you experienced it with them?
- Have you met the people they work with?
- What about their hobbies?
- Do you know why they do what they do, or do you just tolerate it?
- Have you made an effort to get to know your partner's friends, or are they kept separate?

Think about the ways in which your lives are connected and separate. Do you make your relationship a priority? Are there things you can do that would bring you closer? Knowing more about your partner's life will, for example, make it easier for you to give them your support during tough times. That's essential for a healthy relationship, for intimacy and commitment. You'll also appreciate that each of you has individual needs. So, for example, instead of feeling jealous of your partner's work colleagues, why not make an effort to get to know them? Invite them round for a supper or meet up for drinks. Forging a stronger connection makes for more mutual respect and appreciation.

Now try this exercise. On a separate piece of paper, answer the following questions about your partner:

What are your partner's favourite films?
Who was their childhood hero?
Who is their favourite musician?
What would they take to a desert island?
What would they do if they suddenly came into a lot of money?
What are your partner's dreams for the future?
What's their favourite food?
Who is their best friend?
What first attracted you to them?
What would your partner do if they knew they couldn't fail?
What is their greatest fear?
What is their greatest regret?
What makes them feel really happy?

1. Write down the answers YOU think your partner would give to the questions above.
2. Then ask your partner to answer each of the questions.
3. Compare lists with each other.

How close were you? Were you surprised about how little or how much you knew about each other? Don't take a lack of knowledge as criticism; try to see this was a way of learning more about each other, and make a joke of what you've missed rather than seeing it as anyone's fault. If you've learned things you didn't know, list them here or in your journal.

Keeping Your Relationship Healthy: Expressing Affection

Close, caring physical contact releases feel-good chemicals in the brain that help humans bond together. A warm cuddle and a kiss is therefore a very powerful way to bring you closer together, but even so, affection can get easily neglected or pushed aside. Touching and physical closeness are essential parts of any enduring relationship. Use loving gestures like hugging, whispering words of love, touching or smiling warmly whenever you can. Don't just confine them to the bedroom. Do Something Different. Communicate your warm feelings for each other as much as you can and spontaneously

– don't make the mistake of assuming your loved one knows they are loved or doesn't want to keep hearing it. Express your loving feelings regularly in words, simple gestures and tokens of affection.

Acceptance

Although you are in a relationship and may be part of a strong family unit, it's also vital to the health of those relationships that you let others direct their own lives. The best you can do is offer your perspective, make suggestions or offer help if asked. Ultimately, you have to let others decide for themselves. This goes for children, too. If you attempt to force others to think, feel or act in the way *you* think best, you may do more damage than if you were just to allow them the dignity of suffering the consequences of their actions. That way they'll also learn a lot faster and get to know themselves better. And you can relax in the knowledge that you can't orchestrate other people's lives for them.

Even the very closest couples who have lived for decades in marital harmony may have very different views and opinions. Sometimes it's these differences that keep the relationship alive. Provided, that is, that each can respect the other's different view. That means listening to each other respectfully and accepting the difference. If you can come to terms with diversity in your ideas (whether about politics, religion or music) without being critical of each other, it can lead to learning and growth, rather than damaging the relationship.

Make an effort too to distinguish outside issues from personal issues. Don't damage your relationship by letting disagreements about external issues seem like a personal attack. If your partner is on the opposite side of the political spectrum to you, they aren't rejecting you, just holding a different view on one aspect of life. Do Something Different and try to understand why your partner has those beliefs. Where did they come from? If you can, find out why he or she has strong opinions – but remember that not everyone is comfortable with discussing their innermost emotions, so try to respect this difference.

Staying on the Same Wavelength

Sometimes if we are stressed or feeling low, we become preoccupied with our own thoughts and worries. We then risk shutting out our partner and not noticing how they might be feeling. Do Something Different when you're feeling a bit self-absorbed and actively try to defocus from your own thoughts and feelings, and refocus on your partner. Ask them questions about how their day went. What was the best thing that happened today? Or acknowledge when they're having a tough time at work and show appreciation. Being supportive and showing understanding will help keep the lines of communication open, and these qualities are more likely to be reciprocated, or sent back, if you can demonstrate them yourself. Don't pick fights that aren't worth fighting. Ask yourself if it's really important. Learn to let things go and cultivate tolerance.

Being a Team

If you are going through a rocky patch or experiencing relationship problems, it's really important to try to work together toward a compromise. Get outside help if you feel you need it, or discuss how you can sort things out yourselves, together. Whatever you do, don't be deceitful, get angry, play games or try to score points off your partner. Try not to feel you have to 'win'. If either partner 'wins', the relationship loses. Work toward a joint solution.

Joint problem-solving ideas:

- Work toward mutual understanding of the problem.
- Listen, stay focused and stay in the present.
- Choose the right time and place.
- Accept your partner's feelings as *facts*.
- Brainstorm possible solutions together.
- Compromise if necessary.
- Appreciate each other's wants and needs.
- Go for a win-win solution.
- Test it out, being prepared to refine it further and renegotiate.

Better Relationship Habits

When we first meet someone we're on our best behaviour and eager to impress them. Over time, though, and with familiarity, we tend to make less effort and even slip into bad relationship habits. Like lots of other behavioural habits, many of these go on beneath the radar, without us even thinking about them. Perhaps we're less affectionate, too critical or more detached than we used to be? Or maybe we've got into the habit of trading insults, using mockery and hostile humour? You may need to Do Something Different to reverse some of the automatic habits that have put the dampeners on your relationship, especially if you want to bring back the romance.

> **Do Something Different by being aware and not operating on autopilot.**
>
> **Can you spot the things you do and say in your relationship that have just developed as bad habits?**

These might include things like moaning, criticizing, failing to appreciate, blaming, nagging, not listening, etc. Start replacing these with some healthier habits, starting with speaking positively to each other and never, ever saying something you know will harm the other person's feelings.

Here's an example:

> Jane's husband spent the weekend renewing their bathroom. He ripped out the old suite, fitted a new one, laid a new floor and decorated. When Jane's friend asked her how Bob had got on with the bathroom, Jane replied, 'Oh I'm sick of it. He still hasn't finished the tiling!'

Sometimes we forget to appreciate what the other person has done *right* and only notice what they've done *wrong*. How does that make the other person feel?

Many relationships take a turn for the worse because they build up a negative balance. Partners get into the habit of whinging, moaning or saying negative things to each other. When one person is in a moaning mood it's contagious and really drags down the moods of others around them. The person on the receiving end begins to feel unloved or dissatisfied. They fire back a few negative comments of their own. So, remember that moods are contagious. See if you can make an effort to remain upbeat and make a place for love, compassion and joy. Try to get into the good habit of commenting on positive aspects of life that you see or feel. Watch how your positive mood lifts the mood of others.

Sadly, some people find it difficult to say really loving things to another person, even though we all know that criticism hurts. And it's only human to like to hear nice things about ourselves and receive compliments.

Psychologists have identified something called the 5-to-1 rule. That is, it takes *five positive comments* to overcome *one negative comment*. This ratio was first spotted by Gottman when he analyzed the emotions of young men after criticism, particularly when they were criticized by a woman. Male–female relationships where the ratio was as low as one to one (one negative comment for every positive one) had a very low chance of survival.

Do Something Different: The most effective quick-fix for a relationship is to make sure your positive comments to each other outnumber the negative ones by five to one.

First decide what negative relationship habits you might have, and start to 'spot' them in yourself. Of course there might be behaviours that you think your partner needs to change. This process is *not* about changing them, however. They may change if you change, but your focus has to be on you, because you can only change yourself.

> **Do something different – it's the only way to get something different.**

This is all about counting your own positive and negative behaviours in the relationship. Then seeing whether you have a healthy balance.

1. It doesn't matter what the situation is, or how much you think you have been provoked – if you do anything described on the negatives list, it counts as a negative. There are NO exceptions, excuses or extenuating circumstances!
2. It's easier to spot when someone else, and not ourselves, is behaving negatively. Be aware and be honest!
3. LEARN the ten positives and the ten negatives. Or pin them up somewhere to remind you.
4. Remember the 5-to-1 rule: it takes five positives to counteract one negative comment.

10 Positive Relationship Habits
(Check Any You Do Regularly)

Praising your partner	
Expressing your thanks	
Showing your appreciation	
Pointing out your partner's good qualities	
Offering support, help or empathy	
Showing understanding	
Supporting their decisions and goals	
Being affectionate	
Doing something for them or because they want to	
Saying something nice about them to others	

10 Negative Relationship Habits
(Check Any You Do Regularly)

Blaming something on your partner	
Criticizing them or the things they do	
Moaning to them all the time	
Putting them down in any way	
Being disrespectful, name-calling, snapping	
Running them down in front of other people	
Reacting, showing anger, irritation or disdain	
Failing to support their decisions or goals	
Dismissing or not valuing their opinion	
Nagging	

Look at these lists; do you have more checks against the positive habits than the negatives? If so, you're doing really well. You have a harmonious relationship and Cupid has probably taken up residence in your home. More checks against the negatives than positives, though, means love might soon fly out of the window.

Can you talk through the lists with your partner? Look at the negative habits that have crept in but don't blame either person for them. Does your partner agree with you about the balance of positive to negatives? It's important that both partners have a similar view of their relationship – and agree on the 5-to-1 rule.

If your relationship isn't the one you want, perhaps you're doing too many of the negative things and need to change. That means cutting back on the negative comments and introducing more of the positives. Try reframing your daily activities in positive terms, or discovering a positive value in everyday things. Remember to be affectionate, too, and don't think hugs are only for the bedroom.

Remember, you can't expect your partner to change just by wishing it (or nagging them). But if *you* Do Something Different, you will probably get a different reaction back. And it's likely to be a more positive one.

DSD Love Bites

Now that you're turning your attention to Love, not Smoking, here are our Do Something Different love bites – tips to keep your relationship healthy and alive:

- When you feel like criticizing, find something to praise.
- Make time to be a couple.
- Do something nice for the other person.
- Be more positive.
- Remember your first attraction to each other.
- Role-swap a couple of chores.
- Bite your tongue if you can't say something kind.
- Know who your partner's work friends are.
- Give more hugs.
- Notice the little (positive) things.
- Stop comparing who does what and be a team.
- Solve a dispute with rock, paper, scissors.
- Choose the right time to talk.
- Share a hobby or interest.
- Try a new way of communicating (write a letter/ leave a note).
- Learn to laugh off unimportant things.
- Find out more about each other.
- Maintain more eye contact with each other.
- Make an effort for the other person (dress up/ freshen up).
- Smile more.
- Make up silly names for each other.
- Tune out distractions and be present for the other person.
- Balance a negative comment with five positive ones.
- Notice the good things instead of the bad.
- If in doubt, Do Something Different!

POSTSCRIPT

We firmly believe Do Something Different (DSD) is the only way to change. It can help shift attitudes, negative thoughts and unwanted behaviours, the things that hold people back and prevent them from living well.

We want to make a difference. We believe that DSD can do this. Our mission is to bring DSD to as many people as possible, to build a better society where people are happier and more integrated – thinking more healthily, doing what is right and getting what they want.

DSD is based on solid psychological research and theory. It has been applied to a wide range of issues such as changing health behaviours, anxiety and depression, family functioning, bias and diversity, improving relationships, personal development, performance and stress. It is applicable in any situation where people do things on automatic pilot and where habits can turn into problems.

We are dedicated to improving people's lives. We are actively involved in community projects as well as commercial ones, where we design interventions tailored to the unique needs of the organization. Our commercial work helps to make our community-based projects possible. If you want to discuss a potential application of DSD in a commercial context, or if you share a desire to make a contribution and can see the intrinsic value of the **Do Something Different** approach, then contact us at: karenandben@lovenotsmoking.com.

© Ben (C) Fletcher & Karen Pine, 2010

ABOUT THE AUTHORS

Karen Pine and **Ben [C] Fletcher,** the authors of *The No Diet Diet* (with Dr. Danny Penman), are both professors of psychology at the University of Hertfordshire in the UK, and are renowned experts on behavior modification. Their Do Something Different technique has been very successful in helping people lose weight, tackle stress, and improve health and well-being.

Website: **www.lovenotsmoking.com**

INDEX

The initials DSD stand for Love Not Smoking: Do Something Different programme.

NOTES

NOTES

NOTES

NOTES

NOTES

OUR APP

Need a little extra help?

Why not try the
LOVE NOT SMOKING App

Packed with daily tasks,
inspirational ideas, habit-breaking
tools, and twitchy finger game –
this is an app with a difference!!

Available Now for all Devices

facebook ®

Giving up smoking can be a lonely experience.

That's why we've created the **LOVE NOT SMOKING** support network.

Join us on Facebook and meet fellow quitters.

Help each other to give up and stay smoke free.

Why not visit

WWW.LOVENOTSMOKING.COM

for some great extra free tools.

We hope you enjoyed this Hay House book. If you'd like to receive our online catalog featuring additional information on Hay House books and products, or if you'd like to find out more about the Hay Foundation, please contact:

Hay House, Inc., P.O. Box 5100, Carlsbad, CA 92018-5100
(760) 431-7695 or (800) 654-5126
(760) 431-6948 (fax) or (800) 650-5115 (fax)
www.hayhouse.com® • **www.hayfoundation.org**

❊❊

Published and distributed in Australia by: Hay House Australia Pty. Ltd., 18/36 Ralph St., Alexandria NSW 2015 • *Phone:* 612-9669-4299 • *Fax:* 612-9669-4144 • www.hayhouse.com.au

Published and distributed in the United Kingdom by*:* Hay House UK, Ltd., 292B Kensal Rd., London W10 5BE • *Phone:* 44-20-8962-1230 • *Fax:* 44-20-8962-1239 • www.hayhouse.co.uk

Published and distributed in the Republic of South Africa by: Hay House SA (Pty), Ltd., P.O. Box 990, Witkoppen 2068 • *Phone/Fax:* 27-11-467-8904 • www.hayhouse.co.za

Published in India by: Hay House Publishers India, Muskaan Complex, Plot No. 3, B-2, Vasant Kunj, New Delhi 110 070 • *Phone:* 91-11-4176-1620 • *Fax:* 91-11-4176-1630 • www.hayhouse.co.in

Distributed in Canada by*:* Raincoast, 9050 Shaughnessy St., Vancouver, B.C. V6P 6E5 • *Phone:* (604) 323-7100 *Fax:* (604) 323-2600 • www.raincoast.com

❊❊

Take Your Soul on a Vacation

Visit **www.HealYourLife.com**® to regroup, recharge, and reconnect with your own magnificence. Featuring blogs, mind-body-spirit news, and life-changing wisdom from Louise Hay and friends.

Visit **www.HealYourLife.com** today!

Mind Your Body,
Mend Your Spirit

Hay House is the ultimate resource for inspirational and health-conscious books, audio programs, movies, events, e-newsletters, member communities, and much more.

Visit **www.hayhouse.com**® today and nourish your soul.

UPLIFTING EVENTS

Join your favorite authors at live events in a city near you or log on to **www.hayhouse.com** to visit with Hay House authors online during live, interactive Web events.

INSPIRATIONAL RADIO

Daily inspiration while you're at work or at home. Enjoy radio programs featuring your favorite authors, streaming live on the Internet 24/7 at **HayHouseRadio.com**®. Tune in and tune up your spirit!

VIP STATUS

Join the Hay House VIP membership program today and enjoy exclusive discounts on books, CDs, calendars, card decks, and more. You'll also receive 10% off all event reservations (excluding cruises). Visit **www.hayhouse.com/wisdom** to join the Hay House Wisdom Community™.

Visit **www.hayhouse.com** and enter priority code 2723 during checkout for special savings!
(One coupon per customer.)

Heal Your Life One Thought at a Time . . . on Louise's All-New Website!

"Life is bringing me everything I need and more."

— Louise Hay

Come to HEALYOURLIFE.COM today and meet the world's best-selling self-help authors; the most popular leading intuitive, health, and success experts; up-and-coming inspirational writers; and new like-minded friends who will share their insights, experiences, personal stories, and wisdom so you can heal your life and the world around you . . . one thought at a time.

Here are just some of the things you'll get at HealYourLife.com:

- DAILY AFFIRMATIONS
- CAPTIVATING VIDEO CLIPS
- EXCLUSIVE BOOK REVIEWS
- AUTHOR BLOGS
- LIVE TWITTER AND FACEBOOK FEEDS
- BEHIND-THE-SCENES SCOOPS
- LIVE STREAMING RADIO
- "MY LIFE" COMMUNITY OF FRIENDS

PLUS:
FREE Monthly Contests and Polls
FREE BONUS gifts, discounts,
and newsletters

Make It Your Home Page Today!
www.HealYourLife.com®

HEAL YOUR LIFE ♥

3 3132 03170 8409
OKANAGAN REGIONAL L

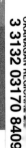